P9-EJI-115

"If there's any teammate I trust in the kitchen, it's my man Shaq! All I can say is . . . pass me a plate!"

—DWYANE WADE
former NBA all-star

"Shaq had me at 'breakfast for dinner.' Get ready to create new family favorites. These easy-to-follow recipes are a slam dunk."

—CARLA HALL
author of *Carla Hall's Soul Food*

SHAQ'S
family style

SHAQ'S
family style

Championship Recipes for
Feeding Family and Friends

SHAQUILLE
O'NEAL

**with Rachel Holtzman, Matthew Silverman,
and Matthew Piekarski**

Photographs by Eva Kolenko

TEN SPEED PRESS
California | New York

CONTENTS

2

M.D.E.—MEALS DONE EASY   41

3

I LOVE PANCAKES—BREAKFAST FOR DINNER   79

4

SANDWICHES ALL DAY—'NUFF SAID 109

5

SHAQ DIESEL—FUEL FOR WHEN YOU WANT THINGS HEALTHY(ISH) 133

6

THE BIG ARISTOTLE—MEALS FOR A CROWD 165

7

IT AIN'T OVER 'TIL THERE'S BANANA PUDDING—DESSERT! 203

Introduction

I know what you might be thinking: What is a basketball Hall-of-Famer doing writing a cookbook? What could I possibly know about food and cooking? Well, I'm gonna tell you something: You don't get to be 7'1", 325, with a 7'4" wingspan and size 22 feet, without knowing a thing or two about how to eat. As I like to say, I got a G-14 classification—the special clearance you get when you've won titles—for knowing a thing or two about a thing or two, and that includes what makes for a good meal.

For a long time, I didn't have to think too much about what I'd be stuffing into this big mouth of mine. I had my sisters and my mom—my job was to look out for them, and they spoiled me and cooked. And they did it well. Mac 'n' cheese, fried chicken, barbecued chicken, banana pudding—they played the hits. Oh, and plenty of spinach, too, because I thought I was Popeye, and it was the only vegetable I'd eat. Even though we didn't have much, we always had good meals. I don't know how my mother did it, but every day was a hell of a breakfast, hell of a school lunch, and hell of a dinner.

Lucille O'Neal was also a stretcher—she knew how to make a lot from a little. She figured out how to take inexpensive ingredients, like eggs and chicken, and change 'em up over the course of the week. Then, when the money would start to run out, we'd go to our safe haven of cereal— especially Frosted Flakes, which remains one of my favorite foods to this day. Just check my pantry (and Frosted Flakes–Crusted French Toast on page 93 and Frosted Flakes–Chocolate Chip Cookies on page 213). And there'd be, like, ten pounds of sugar in the house at all times, so we could get as much mileage out of our lemonade as possible. But no matter what, our mama never made us feel like there wasn't enough to go around, and there was always room for more people at the table. You may wonder where this physique came from, but take one look at my mother and you know who is responsible for this big ol' heart.

I like to say that what keeps me motivated is my MBA—mama, babies, and associates. I've got my brother and sisters, cousins, aunts and uncles, nephews and nieces, six beautiful children with two beautiful women, plus teammates, friends, and partners who, along with their families, have become like relatives over the years. I take care of this crew in all kinds of ways, and you know there's gonna be a good meal to go along with it;

whether it's people stopping by to watch the game, having a barbecue, grabbing some breakfast, or just kicking back. And now that I'm middle-aged, I finally realized it was time for me to contribute in the kitchen. I thought, *You know what? I gotta learn how to cook*. I want my mom to officially hang up her apron, retire her number, put her feet up, and watch *General Hospital*. And I wanna cook for my kids. Growing up, they knew three things: 1. Never interrupt Daddy's nap on game day. 2. My love for them is unconditional—forever and always. 3. If you want to touch my cheese, you have to get three degrees—a bachelor's, master's, and doctorate or JD. And now they also know, especially thanks to spending most of the year 2020 together 24-7, that I've got them covered in the kitchen too.

When it came to learning how to cook—something that's not exactly easy, considering my schedule—I knew that I had to give the process a Shaqification. I may have a doctoral degree in education, but I have never claimed to be the smartest guy in the room. So, I became an expert at taking things that are difficult and breaking them down into simpler parts. It started back when I was in school—When did Columbus arrive in America? I couldn't memorize it, so I made up a little song—*1492, this is what we gotta do; 1492, this is what we gotta do*. I took the information and made it work for me. The same went for basketball. You know how I learned to play ball? By watching the greats, like Alonzo Mourning, Bill Russell, Hakeem Olajuwon, Isiah Thomas, Julius "Dr. J" Erving, and Wilt Chamberlain. How did I learn how to cook? Same thing—from watching the all-stars: my mama, my executive chefs Matt Silverman and Matt Piekarski, and my personal chef Alex Conant. I couldn't do the real fast *boom boom boom boom* that the chefs do; so once again, I figured out how to make it work for me. I'm real good at following directions, so I asked for a bunch of simple recipes that were full of the flavor, which my mother taught me and in which I've since received an honorary chef's degree from all the eating I've done throughout my life. With those basics, I realized I could do some pretty good work. And the same will go for you—it's like anything else in life: the more reps you get in, the better you become.

The mission to tighten up my kitchen skills is also what led me to develop my line of appliances—so I could just press a button, walk away, talk to my kids, maybe have a Strawberry Shaquiri, and *ding*, get dinner on the table. Can you make these recipes without these time-saving, strong move-making, love life–improving appliances? Most definitely. But do I think everyone's kitchen is better with a little Shaq in it? Damn straight I do.

But this book really is about the food. When it came time to think of titles for it, I first wanted to call it *Recipes for Dummies,* because that's how easy I wanted the methods to be. But then I thought, maybe, *Shaq-a-Nova,* because I wanted to show all those young people out there how important and easy it is to do something helpful around the house. But, then, the obvious right choice came along: *Shaq's Family Style,* because if you're making these meals for your loved ones, even if it's just one or two nights a week, you're winning.

The recipes you'll find here are inspired by a combination of things: mostly recipes I know I can make (as in, not very difficult), things from my childhood (pancakes, fried chicken, barbecue chicken, mac 'n' cheese, banana pudding, Oreos), things I love to eat (pancakes, fried chicken, barbecue chicken, mac 'n' cheese, banana pudding, Oreos), places I've been (loaded waffles from Atlanta, St. Louis-style ribs, Louisiana jambalaya), people I love (my mama's meatloaf, spaghetti and meatballs), things I believe in (like the kind of great meat you can get from Meat District and put in everything from tamale pie to smash burgers), and, of course, some of my world-famous inventions (Smack Ramen, Big Chicken, *thammiches*—not to be confused with sandwiches). And they are going to have you covered for every meal of the day, whether it's just you and your family, or the whole neighborhood getting together. I even threw in some recipes for when you want to keep things a little bit healthier. I can't say that it's what I'm about 100 percent of the time, but I do know how important it is to balance some of those shrimp and grits and chicken tenders with things on the lighter side, so you don't end up with a BOTB—Barkley over the Belt. These recipes are more exciting than the whitefish and asparagus diet that my trainer Roc Shabazz once tried to keep me on, but they'll still have you looking just as strong as me. But really, anything made with from-scratch ingredients is a heck of a lot better than anything you get going to the drive-thru or heating up from a package.

Okay, enough talkin'—it's officially game time. So, grab your apron, grab your whisk, maybe give yourself a little pump-up speech in the mirror, hear the fans chanting your name, and get into that kitchen. And don't forget to send me an invite for dinner sometime; just make sure there's chicken.

A Few Notes from the Matts

As Shaquille's executive chef partners for the past eight years, we've not only gotten pretty good at figuring out what kind of food people want to eat but, thanks to Shaquille's drive to learn how to cook, we've also figured out how to set up someone for success in the kitchen.

The recipes in this book will deliver a ton of flavor while not demanding a lot of time or effort. We've also included plenty of tips for how to make a recipe work better for you with suggestions for things such as ingredient substitutions or alternative cooking methods.

Before you get started, here are a few things we'd like to point out about our cooking philosophy that will make your cooking better, easier, and less expensive.

» No more "season to taste." A lot of cookbooks will simply tell you to season something "to taste" with salt and pepper. But that doesn't really mean a whole lot to someone who's just getting comfortable in the kitchen. What's the point of a recipe if it's, ultimately, going to make you do the guesswork? Instead, we've made sure that every recipe provides its own specific seasoning amounts. That will help you get solid, consistent results and, over time, get the hang of how to properly season food.

» Introducing freshly ground black pepper. It's time to step away from the pre-ground stuff. Grinding black peppercorns as you need them, whether it's with a built-in grinder, a blender, a manual pepper mill, or the Shaq Gravity Spice Mill, is not only easy but it also makes a big difference in how much flavor you introduce to a dish.

» Our new secret weapon is *evaporated milk*. Normally, recipes call for heavy cream to add richness to such dishes as sauces, casseroles, and other creamy items. But cream, thanks to its high fat content, can be very expensive and is very perishable. Most people don't have much use for cream once they've used some for a recipe, so it oftentimes gets thrown out. So, for this book, for the majority of recipes that might otherwise use heavy cream, we call for evaporated milk instead. It's shelf-stable, inexpensive, has a fraction of the calories and fat as cream, and comes in a handy can size that lends itself to single-use portions—so there's no waste. And yet, it'll give you the same satisfyingly decadent consistency that cream does.

This is from-scratch cooking. By that, we mean the recipes call for plenty of wholesome ingredients, all easily found at your neighborhood grocery and that go together quickly.

1

THAT'S

BARBECUE CHICKEN

all the hits

During my time as an analyst on *Inside the NBA*, I've been known to issue "Barbecue Chicken Alerts"—that's when a player is gonna smoke another player. It's a player who's the truth, looking at his opponent like he's something you can cook, roast, and eat up *all* game. *That's barbecue chicken!*

These meals are the same thing—they're the real deal and the ones that'll have you lickin' your fingers every time. Plus, there also happens to actually be a lot of chicken—and that's no accident. Growing up, chicken was the main event on the menu because it was inexpensive and my mother knew how to spread it out. She'd buy a big bag at the beginning of the week and, the first day, she'd bake it up, the second day she'd fry it up, and the third day, maybe she'd add a little barbecue sauce to it. There were no complaints from me—chicken is, to *this* day, one of my favorite foods and the inspiration behind my Big Chicken restaurants. And I owe it all to my mama, the original Barbecue Chicken MVP.

Slow-Cooker Southern Mac 'n' Cheese

MAKES 8 SERVINGS

Here's a Lucille O'Neal classic and, probably, one of my favorite things to eat. She called it "Li'l Shaq's Easy Mac"; and when I was a kid, she made it for me after every game. Now, no matter how healthy I'm trying to eat, I will always love being treated to a big ol' bowl of mac. You've made this right if you get those unbreakable cheese strings when you take a scoop from the pan.

1 pound elbow pasta

1 pound Velveeta, cut into ½-inch cubes

3 cups whole milk

1½ cups evaporated milk

¼ cup unsalted butter

1 tablespoon kosher salt

1 teaspoon freshly ground black pepper

1 cup shredded sharp cheddar cheese

Lightly coat the insert of a 6-quart slow cooker with nonstick cooking spray. In the prepared insert, combine the pasta, Velveeta, whole milk, evaporated milk, butter, salt, and pepper and mix well to incorporate. Cover the slow cooker and turn the heat to high. Cook, covered, for 2 hours, stirring every 30 minutes or so. Top the pasta with the cheddar, replace the cover, and cook for 20 minutes.

Serve the mac immediately.

Put Away and Replay
Store the mac in a sealed container in the fridge for up to 4 days. Reheat in a microwave on high power for 2 minutes, or until heated through.

Note from the Matts

After the mac is done cooking, you could scoop it into a casserole dish and broil until the cheese is bubbly and brown. If you would prefer to use an electric skillet instead of a slow cooker, combine the ingredients as directed, cover, and cook at 200°F for about 45 minutes. Add the cheese as instructed and cover until melted. Serve right out of the skillet.

Cheeseburger Mac
with Crispy Garlic–Parmesan Roasted Broccoli

MAKES 6 SERVINGS

CHEESEBURGER MAC

2 pounds 80/20 ground beef

1 yellow onion,
finely chopped

2 teaspoons minced garlic

1 tablespoon kosher salt

1 teaspoon freshly ground
black pepper

1 pound elbow pasta

1 pound Velveeta, cut into
1-inch pieces

4 cups 2% milk

1½ cups evaporated milk

1 cup ketchup

1 cube beef bouillon

1 cup shredded
cheddar cheese

CRISPY GARLIC–
PARMESAN ROASTED
BROCCOLI

8 cups fresh broccoli florets

½ cup extra-virgin olive oil

1 cup grated
Parmesan cheese

16 saltines, finely ground

2 tablespoons minced garlic

2 teaspoons kosher salt

1 teaspoon freshly ground
black pepper

I'm not sure there's a better meal out there (except maybe pancakes with grape jelly)—two of my favorite things mashed up together served with some crisp little cheesy broccoli bits that make even me want to eat my vegetables.

Pro Move

When coating the broccoli, you can cover the bowl with one the same size (upside down), hold the bowls together firmly, and shake vigorously. Or, put a larger bowl over the top, then hold them together and shake to get things nice and coated.

To make the cheeseburger mac: In a large nonstick pan over medium-high heat, cook the ground beef, breaking it up with the back of a wooden spoon, for about 8 minutes, or until browned and no longer pink. Add the onion and garlic and cook for 5 minutes more, or until the onion is translucent. Season with the salt and pepper.

Transfer the beef to the insert of a slow cooker and stir in the pasta, Velveeta, 2% milk, evaporated milk, ketchup, and bouillon cube. Cover the cooker, turn the heat to high, and cook for 2 hours, stirring every 30 minutes. Top the beef with the cheddar, replace the cover, and cook for another 20 minutes.

continued ▶

Cheeseburger Mac with Crispy Garlic–Parmesan Roasted Broccoli

CONTINUED

To make the broccoli: Preheat the oven to 400°F. Line a baking sheet with aluminum foil.

In a large bowl, combine the broccoli and olive oil and toss to coat. Add the Parmesan, saltines, garlic, salt, and pepper and toss well to coat evenly.

Spread the broccoli on the prepared baking sheet, scraping out any crumbs remaining in the mixing bowl and sprinkling them over the broccoli. Roast for 20 minutes, or until the broccoli is golden brown.

Serve the cheeseburger mac with the broccoli on the side.

Put Away and Replay

Store the mac and broccoli in separate sealed containers in the fridge for up to 2 days. Reheat each in a microwave on high power for 2 minutes, or until heated through.

Notes from the Matts

After the mac is done cooking, scoop it into a casserole dish or oven-proof skillet and broil until the cheese is bubbly and brown. Or, make the cheeseburger mac in an electric skillet. After browning the meat, add the remaining ingredients, cover, and cook at 200°F for about 45 minutes. Add the cheese as instructed and cover until melted. You could also sprinkle some chopped crispy bacon over the top to make this Bacon Cheeseburger Mac.

Carolina BBQ Shrimp and Buttery Cheese Grits

MAKES 6 SERVINGS

I don't care how sophisticated you want to feel cooking at home—if you want to eat well, forget all that foo-foo nonsense. You don't need caviar or frilly stuff or ingredients you can't pronounce. To me, it doesn't matter how fancy a meal is, it should always include comforting, stick-to-your-ribs, remember-to-call-your-mama kinda food, just like shrimp and grits.

In a large resealable plastic bag or large mixing bowl, mix together the shrimp, ¼ cup olive oil, Cajun spice, and garlic. Seal the bag and let marinate in the fridge for 30 minutes.

To make the grits: In a large saucepan over medium-high heat, combine the water, 2% milk, butter, salt, and pepper. Bring the mixture to a boil, whisk in the grits, and cook for 5 minutes, stirring constantly. Remove the pan from the heat and stir in the cheddar and cream cheese. Let the grits stand for 5 minutes to thicken.

In a medium bowl, whisk together the chicken broth, mustard, ketchup, vinegar, brown sugar, Worcestershire, and lemon juice. Set this sauce aside.

Pour the 2 tablespoons olive oil into a large skillet over high heat. Add the onion and both bell peppers and cook for 3 minutes, or until the onion is translucent.

continued ▶

2 pounds shell-off, tail-off shrimp, fresh or frozen and thawed (see Note)

¼ cup extra-virgin olive oil

2 tablespoons Cajun Spice (see page 35)

1 tablespoon minced garlic

BUTTERY CHEESE GRITS

4 cups water

2 cups 2% milk

½ cup unsalted butter

1 tablespoon kosher salt

2 teaspoons freshly ground black pepper

1½ cups quick-cooking grits (see Note)

1 cup shredded cheddar cheese

8 ounces plain cream cheese

½ cup chicken broth

½ cup yellow mustard

¼ cup ketchup

¼ cup apple cider vinegar

Carolina BBQ Shrimp and Buttery Cheese Grits

CONTINUED

Remove the shrimp from the marinade and add them to the skillet. Cook the shrimp, stirring continuously, for about 2 minutes, or until they're just turning firm and pink and are no longer translucent. Any longer and they will be overcooked and rubbery. Add the reserved sauce to the skillet and remove from the heat. Add the butter and stir to incorporate, so the sauce thickens.

Pour the grits into a casserole dish or individual bowls, top with the shrimp and scallions, and serve immediately.

Put Away and Replay
Store the grits and shrimp in separate sealed containers in the fridge for up to 3 days. To reheat the grits, add a small amount of milk to a saucepan over medium heat and bring it to a simmer. Turn the heat to low, add the grits, and stir for about 10 minutes, or until heated through. Reheating the shrimp is not recommended since they'll likely overcook, and the butter will separate from the sauce. They'll warm through enough once they're tossed into the reheated grits.

2 tablespoons packed light brown sugar

2 tablespoons Worcestershire sauce

2 tablespoons fresh lemon juice

2 tablespoons extra-virgin olive oil

1 large yellow onion, chopped

1 large red bell pepper, seeded and chopped

1 large green bell pepper, seeded and chopped

½ cup unsalted butter

½ cup chopped scallions, white and green parts

Notes from the Matts

You can use any size shrimp you like; just remember that smaller ones need less time to cook, and larger ones need more. No matter what, don't overcook the shrimp. You could also use stone-ground grits instead of instant. Follow the package instructions to adjust the cooking time. For the grits, add 1 cup canned roasted chopped green chiles for even more texture and flavor; just fold them in at the end.

Smack Ramen Chicken Alfredo

MAKES 6 SERVINGS

3 cups evaporated milk

3 cups 2% milk

¼ cup unsalted butter

6 (3-ounce) packages chicken-flavored ramen noodles

1 teaspoon kosher salt

1 teaspoon garlic powder

½ teaspoon onion powder

½ teaspoon freshly ground black pepper

¼ teaspoon hot sauce (preferably Tabasco or Crystal)

8 ounces frozen chopped broccoli

1 pound shredded rotisserie chicken (do yourself a favor and go with one from the store)

½ cup grated Parmesan cheese

3 egg yolks (optional)

I was lucky enough to grow up with a lot of women looking out for me, spoiling me, and feeding me great food. I never really had a need to teach myself to cook, so when I went to college, it was all about what you might refer to as Top Ramen but what I call "Smack Ramen"—'cause it was so good it was a smackdown. For this recipe, you're doing a little bit more than just adding hot water and those little flavor packets to the noodles, but it only takes 10 minutes and is so easy that even Charles Barkley could do it.

Pro Move

You'll have leftover flavor packets after you make this, but save them for adding that smack factor to soup, pasta, eggs, what have you.

In a large nonstick pot over medium-high heat, whisk together the evaporated milk, 2% milk, butter, two of the ramen seasoning packets, salt, garlic powder, onion powder, pepper, and hot sauce. Bring the mixture to a boil, stirring constantly with a spatula or wooden spoon. Be careful; evaporated milk scorches very easily and milk boils over quickly.

When the mixture boils, add all the ramen noodles and continue to stir for 2 to 3 minutes, or until the noodles are cooked through. Add the broccoli and continue to cook, stirring, for 1 minute more, then remove the pot from the heat.

continued ▶

Smack Ramen Chicken Alfredo

Stir the chicken and Parmesan into the pot, followed by the egg yolks (if using)—stirring them in quickly. Let the mixture sit, uncovered, for 2 minutes more before serving.

Put Away and Replay
Store the ramen in a sealed container in the fridge for up to 3 days. Reheat in a microwave on high power for 2 minutes, or until heated through.

Note from the Matts

Adding the egg yolks to the pot in the last step of the recipe makes the Alfredo sauce even richer. Make sure you stir them in quickly, so they don't scramble.

Fried Chicken Tenders with Creamy BBQ Dip

MAKES 6 SERVINGS

CREAMY BBQ DIP

1½ cups mayonnaise

⅔ cup ketchup

½ cup packed
light brown sugar

2 tablespoons
apple cider vinegar

2 tablespoons chipotle-
flavor hot sauce
(preferably Tabasco)

1½ teaspoons kosher salt

FRIED CHICKEN TENDERS

18 chicken tenderloins

1½ cups buttermilk

1 tablespoon seasoning salt

Canola oil for frying

1 cup all-purpose flour

36 saltine crackers,
finely ground

1 tablespoon Cajun Spice
(see page 35)

1 tablespoon freshly ground
black pepper

1 teaspoon baking powder

When I was playing in the NBA and would get home late after a game, I'd go right for the fried chicken drummies (or Frosted Flakes, but that's another recipe for another time). These are better than anything you could pull out of the freezer, especially when you throw some BBQ dip into the mix. If you're like me, you're gonna take down about fifty of 'em.

To make the dip: In a medium bowl, whisk together the mayo, ketchup, brown sugar, vinegar, hot sauce, and salt until thoroughly combined. Transfer to a sealed container and refrigerate for up to 1 week.

To prepare the chicken tenders: Place the chicken in a resealable plastic bag. In a medium bowl, whisk together the buttermilk and seasoning salt, then pour the mixture over the chicken. Seal the bag and refrigerate for at least 4 hours, but ideally overnight. Remove the chicken from the fridge and let sit at room temperature for 30 minutes.

Line a baking sheet with a double layer of paper towels. In a fryer, deep skillet, Dutch oven, or large pot over medium-high heat, warm 4 inches of canola oil to 350°F. In a shallow baking dish, whisk together the flour, crackers, Cajun spice, pepper, and baking powder.

continued ▶

Fried Chicken Tenders with Creamy BBQ Dip

CONTINUED

One at a time, remove the marinated chicken tenders from the bag, letting any excess buttermilk drip back into the bag, and place in the flour mixture. Coat well on both sides, gently pressing down to ensure they're covered thoroughly.

Working in batches, fry the tenders for 3 minutes, or until the interior temperature of the chicken registers 165°F on an instant-read thermometer and the crust is golden brown. Transfer to the prepared baking sheet to drain.

Serve the tenders immediately with the creamy BBQ dip.

Put Away and Replay

Store the tenders in a sealed container or resealable plastic bag in the fridge for up to 3 days. Reheat in a 350°F air fryer for about 5 minutes, or in a 350°F oven for 6 to 8 minutes, or just until hot. You can also freeze the fried tenders and reheat this way as well.

Note from the Matts

If you don't have tenderloins, cut chicken breasts into strips.

Sheet Pan BBQ Chicken Thighs with Sweet Potato Bake

MAKES 6 SERVINGS

When I say this is gonna be barbecue chicken, I mean it's *gonna be barbecue chicken*—it's going to deliver when it counts. Can't you just picture those juicy chicken thighs gettin' all slathered in their sauce that gets all caramelized and crispy in the oven? Served over some sweet potatoes that don't know whether they're a dessert or a vegetable? Excuse me for a minute while I go find something to eat. . . .

Pro Move

Want to substitute other cuts of chicken—legs, breasts, wings—for thighs? Don't know why you would, but you do you. Just be sure to give yourself time to let them marinate overnight to let all that flavor get nice and cozy with the chicken.

To marinate the chicken: In a medium bowl, whisk together the ketchup, brown sugar, vinegar, Worcestershire, honey, chipotles in adobo, mustard, salt, pepper, garlic powder, and onion powder to make a marinade.

Place the chicken thighs in a large resealable plastic bag and pour in the marinade. Seal the bag and make sure the chicken is coated. Refrigerate for at least 4 hours, but ideally overnight.

continued ▶

SHEET PAN BBQ CHICKEN THIGHS

2½ cups ketchup

½ cup packed light brown sugar

¼ cup apple cider vinegar

¼ cup Worcestershire sauce

¼ cup honey

¼ cup chipotles in adobo

¼ cup yellow mustard

1 tablespoon kosher salt

1 tablespoon freshly ground black pepper

2 teaspoons garlic powder

2 teaspoons onion powder

12 bone-in, skin-on chicken thighs

Sheet Pan BBQ Chicken Thighs with Sweet Potato Bake

CONTINUED

To make the sweet potato bake: Preheat the oven to 350°F.

Prick the sweet potatoes with the tines of a fork, wrap each in aluminum foil, and place them on a baking sheet. Bake for 1 hour, until very soft when pierced with a knife or a fork. Let the sweet potatoes rest until they're cool enough to handle. Keep the oven on.

Peel the sweet potatoes and discard the skins. Place the flesh in a large mixing bowl; add ¾ cup of the brown sugar, the orange zest, orange juice, and melted butter; and mix well. Lightly coat a 9 by 13-inch casserole dish with nonstick cooking spray and add the sweet potato mixture.

In a medium bowl, combine the pecans, oats, flour, remaining ½ cup brown sugar, cold cubed butter, cinnamon, salt, and ginger and mix well, using your hands if needed to work the butter into the rest of the mixture, until uniform and crumbly. Spread the pecan mixture over the sweet potatoes.

Bake the sweet potatoes, uncovered, for 40 minutes, or until hot all the way through and the topping is browned. Cover with aluminum foil to keep warm.

To cook the chicken, line a rimmed baking sheet with foil.

In a medium bowl, combine the sliced onion and olive oil and toss to coat. Spread the onion over the prepared baking sheet. Remove the chicken thighs from the bag, letting any excess marinade drip back into the bag. Place the chicken thighs skin-side up on top of the onion in a single layer. Reserve the marinade.

continued ▶

SWEET POTATO BAKE

6 sweet potatoes

1¼ cups packed light brown sugar

2 oranges; peel grated for 2 teaspoons zest and flesh squeezed for ⅔ cup juice

¼ cup melted unsalted butter, plus ⅓ cup cold unsalted butter, cut into small cubes

1 cup chopped pecans

½ cup old-fashioned rolled oats

½ cup all-purpose flour

2 teaspoons ground cinnamon

1 teaspoon kosher salt

¼ teaspoon ground ginger

1 yellow onion, thinly sliced

¼ cup extra-virgin olive oil

Sheet Pan BBQ Chicken Thighs with Sweet Potato Bake

CONTINUED

Bake the chicken for 45 minutes, or until the internal temperature registers 165°F on an instant-read thermometer. Remove the baking sheet from the oven and brush the reserved marinade over the chicken. Turn the broiler to high and place the chicken under the broiler for 5 minutes, or until it's nicely browned. Let the chicken rest for 5 minutes.

Serve the chicken hot, with the sweet potato bake alongside.

Put Away and Replay
Store the chicken and sweet potatoes in separate sealed containers in the fridge for up to 3 days. Reheat each in a microwave on high power for 2 minutes, or until heated through.

Note from the Matts

Feel free to buy your favorite barbecue sauce instead of making this "no-cook" version.

Best Buttermilk Fried Chicken Thighs

MAKES 6 SERVINGS

My mom taught a master class in fried chicken almost every week, which was why, when I opened my Big Chicken restaurants, I wanted it to be her recipe front and center on those buns. This is a little bit of a twist since it's thighs—my personal favorite—instead of breasts, but no matter what you put this spiced breading on, you're gonna send love notes to Mama O'Neal.

Pro Move

If you let the chicken marinate overnight and then sit at room temperature for 30 minutes *before* breading, you'll get more flavorful meat and a crispier outside because you won't be cooling down your oil with a bunch of cold chicken. Timing matters here, so don't get greedy.

5 cups buttermilk

5 tablespoons seasoning salt

12 bone-in, skin-on chicken thighs

5 cups all-purpose or Wondra flour (see Note)

2 tablespoons baking powder

1 tablespoon ground white pepper

1 tablespoon freshly ground black pepper

1 tablespoon garlic powder

1 tablespoon onion powder

1 tablespoon ground mustard

1 teaspoon cayenne pepper

Peanut or canola oil for frying (see Note)

In a medium bowl, whisk together the buttermilk and 3 tablespoons of the seasoning salt. Place the chicken in a large resealable plastic bag and pour in the seasoned buttermilk. Seal the bag and make sure the chicken is evenly coated. Refrigerate for at least 4 hours, but ideally overnight.

In a large bowl, whisk together the flour, baking powder, remaining 2 tablespoons seasoning salt, white pepper, black pepper, garlic powder, onion powder, ground mustard, and cayenne. Transfer the mixture to a shallow baking dish.

continued ▶

Best Buttermilk Fried Chicken Thighs

CONTINUED

Remove the chicken thighs from the buttermilk mixture, letting any excess buttermilk drip back into the bag. Place the chicken in the flour mixture and coat well, pressing firmly to make sure the breading sticks. Let the chicken sit for 15 minutes at room temperature; the breading should become slightly tacky and sticky. Then dredge the chicken in the breading one more time to coat well.

In a fryer, Dutch oven, or large pot over medium-high heat, warm 4 inches of oil to 310°F. Set a wire rack on a baking sheet or line a baking sheet with a double layer of paper towels.

Working in batches of three or four, add the chicken thighs to the oil and fry for 10 to 12 minutes, flipping halfway through the cooking time, until golden brown and the internal temperature registers 165°F on an instant-read thermometer. Transfer the chicken to the prepared baking sheet. (If you like, keep the baking sheet in a 200°F oven to keep the chicken warm—just make sure you prop open the oven door, so the chicken doesn't get soggy.) Let the chicken rest and cool slightly for 5 minutes.

Serve the chicken warm, room temperature, or cold.

Put Away and Replay
Store the chicken in a sealed container in the fridge for up to 3 days. Reheat in a 300°F air fryer for about 20 minutes, or in a 300°F oven for about 25 minutes, or just until hot.

Notes from the Matts

Wondra flour will get you an even better crust consistency than all-purpose flour. And peanut oil makes for better-tasting fried chicken, if allergies aren't an issue.

Southern Glazed Bacon-Wrapped Meatloaf with Creamed Corn Casserole

MAKES 6 SERVINGS

My mom's meatloaf is world-famous. Part of what makes it so special is that she figured out a way to make just a few pounds of beef stretch, so it could feed a lot of people—her four kids plus anyone else who came to dinner, because we were always having guests. I like to level up my meatloaf with primo ground beef from Meat District. A lot of people mess around with brown gravy for their meatloaf, but not Mama—it was tomato sauce all the way. So, the Shaqloaf twist is a tomato glaze with a secret ingredient to bring out that *mmm-mmm* tangy sweetness.

Pro Move

Make the Cajun spice mix to level-up your meatloaf. Once it's in your cupboard, I guarantee you'll want to use it to season plenty of other things, from steaks to chicken to shrimp. If you prefer to skip making the seasoning from scratch, you can substitute any store-bought Cajun spice mix.

To make the Cajun spice: In a medium bowl, stir together the salt, smoked paprika, cayenne, garlic powder, onion powder, white pepper, black pepper, thyme, and oregano. Store in an airtight container or jar at room temperature for up to 1 month.

To make the creamed corn casserole: Preheat the oven to 375°F.

Pour ¼ cup of the melted butter into a 9 by 13-inch casserole dish and set aside.

continued ▶

CAJUN SPICE

¼ cup kosher salt

¼ cup smoked paprika

2 tablespoons cayenne pepper

1 tablespoon garlic powder

1 tablespoon onion powder

1 tablespoon ground white pepper

1 tablespoon freshly ground black pepper

1 tablespoon dried thyme

1 tablespoon dried oregano

CREAMED CORN CASSEROLE

¾ cup melted unsalted butter

4 cups frozen corn kernels; 3 cups thawed, 1 cup left frozen

1½ cups buttermilk

8 ounces plain cream cheese

2 eggs

½ cup cornmeal

½ cup granulated sugar

1 (1.5-ounce) package ranch dressing mix

2 teaspoons baking powder

2 teaspoons kosher salt

1 teaspoon freshly ground black pepper

1 cup shredded cheddar cheese (or goat cheese)

That's Barbecue Chicken

Southern Glazed Bacon-Wrapped Meatloaf with Creamed Corn Casserole

CONTINUED

In a blender, combine the remaining ½ cup melted butter, 3 cups thawed corn, buttermilk, cream cheese, and eggs. Blend until completely smooth, stopping every so often, if needed, to scrape down the sides with a spatula and get rid of any lumps.

In a large bowl, whisk together the cornmeal, sugar, ranch dressing mix, baking powder, salt, and black pepper. Pour the wet mixture from the blender into the dry mixture in the bowl and stir until they just come together. Stir in the cheddar and remaining 1 cup frozen corn. Pour the batter into the prepared casserole dish.

Bake the casserole, uncovered, for 1 hour. If the top gets too brown, cover the dish with aluminum foil for the remaining cooking time. The casserole should be slightly spongy when cooked, and a knife inserted into the middle should come out clean. Cover the casserole with foil to keep warm.

To make the meatloaf: Preheat the oven to 350°F.

Lightly coat a 10-cup Bundt pan with nonstick cooking spray. (You can also do this with two loaf pans, or make a free-form loaf on a baking sheet.) Line a baking sheet with foil and place a wire rack on top.

With one end of each bacon slice at the center of the prepared pan and the other end hanging over the edge of the pan, line the pan with the bacon so the pieces overlap slightly. Set aside.

In a large mixing bowl, whisk together the eggs and whole milk. Add the white bread, mix well, and let the mixture sit for 10 minutes. Then add the ground beef, saltines, onion, ketchup, salt, Cajun spice, Worcestershire, ground mustard, and garlic powder. Mix just until combined.

continued ▶

BACON-WRAPPED MEATLOAF

1 pound sliced bacon

4 eggs

¾ cup whole milk

4 slices white bread, crusts trimmed, cut into cubes

3 pounds 80/20 ground beef

16 saltine crackers, finely ground

½ cup finely grated yellow onion

½ cup ketchup

2 tablespoons kosher salt

1 tablespoon Cajun Spice

1 tablespoon Worcestershire sauce

1 teaspoon ground mustard

1 teaspoon garlic powder

SOUTHERN GLAZE

½ cup grape jelly

1 cup ketchup

1 teaspoon Cajun Spice

Southern Glazed Bacon-Wrapped Meatloaf with Creamed Corn Casserole

CONTINUED

Add the meat mixture to the prepared pan. Pull the overhanging bacon around both sides of the meat and press down firmly but gently to compact it. Place the pan in a 12-inch square baking dish and fill the dish with 1½ inches of water. (If you don't have a square baking dish, place the pan on a rimmed baking sheet to catch any drippings.) Cover the entire Bundt pan and square pan with aluminum foil—this will keep the meatloaf moist during cooking.

Bake the meatloaf for 80 minutes (70 minutes for loaf pans), or until the internal temperature registers 155°F on an instant-read thermometer.

To make the glaze: In a medium microwave-safe bowl, microwave the jelly for 30 seconds on high power, just to melt it. Add the ketchup and Cajun spice and mix well. Set aside.

When the meatloaf is done cooking, pour off any juices and carefully flip the Bundt pan onto the prepared rack to unmold. Pour 1 cup of the glaze over the meatloaf. Turn the oven temperature to 400°F and return the glazed meatloaf to the oven for 20 minutes. For the last 10 minutes of cooking time, return the creamed corn casserole to the oven to warm. Coat the meatloaf a second time with the remaining glaze.

Serve slices of meatloaf with a scoop of the corn casserole on the side.

Put Away and Replay

Store the meatloaf and corn casserole in separate sealed containers in the fridge for up to 4 days. To reheat, place the sliced meatloaf in a baking dish with ¼ inch of water or chicken broth. Cover with foil and bake in a 350°F oven for 30 minutes, or until heated through. The corn casserole can be reheated along with the meatloaf in the oven, or in a microwave on high power for 2 minutes, or until heated through.

"I owe it all to my mama, the original Barbecue Chicken MVP."

2

meals done easy

What can I say, I have a thing for nicknames, especially my own. I've knighted myself the Big Aristotle because the wise man once said excellence is not a singular act, it's a habit—which I truly believe helped me earn the 2000 MVP Award and other wins on and off the court.

I was Big Felon after I made a game-winning steal against the Orlando Magic, and I added the Big Sidekick to the list when I helped the Lakers and Miami Heat win championships. One of the best nicknames I've ever had—M.D.E. or "Most Dominant Ever"—means something totally different in the kitchen. And, no, I'm not referring to Most Dominant Eater.

Southern-Style Turkey Chili with Cheddar Cornbread Waffles

MAKES 6 SERVINGS

I used to be mainly a pancake guy, but after moving to Atlanta—where waffles are more popular than pancakes—I came around to waffles. There's just something about them . . . they're the next-best thing to eating with your hands, like perfect scooping mitts. Add some cheese in there and pile a whole bunch of smoky chili on top? You got yourself a winner-winner turkey dinner.

To make the chili: In a large pot over medium-high heat, warm the olive oil. Add the ground turkey and cook, breaking it up with the back of a wooden spoon, for about 5 minutes, or until the meat is lightly browned. Add the onion and bell pepper and cook for 3 to 4 minutes, until the onion is translucent and the turkey is no longer pink. Stir in the tomato paste and cook, while stirring, for 1 minute. Pour in the chicken broth, tomatoes with juices, green chiles, chili powder, smoked paprika, salt, black pepper, garlic powder, cumin, and cayenne and stir well to combine. Bring to a boil, then turn the heat to low and let simmer.

In the bowl of a food processor, combine the kidney beans and black beans and pulse three or four times, until the beans are very roughly chopped. Be careful not to puree. Add the beans to the pot and stir well. Cover and simmer the chili, stirring occasionally, for 45 minutes to 1 hour, until thickened to your liking.

continued ▶

SOUTHERN-STYLE TURKEY CHILI

2 tablespoons extra-virgin olive oil

2 pounds ground turkey

1 large yellow onion, diced

1 large red bell pepper, seeded and diced

1 (6-ounce) can tomato paste

2 cups chicken broth

2 (14.5-ounce) cans fire-roasted diced tomatoes, with juices

2 (4-ounce) cans mild diced green chilies, drained

¼ cup plus 1 tablespoon chili powder

2 tablespoons smoked paprika

1 tablespoon kosher salt

2 teaspoons freshly ground black pepper

2 teaspoons garlic powder

1 teaspoon ground cumin

1 teaspoon cayenne pepper

1 (15-ounce) can kidney beans, drained and rinsed

1 (15-ounce) can black beans, drained and rinsed

Southern-Style Turkey Chili with Cheddar Cornbread Waffles

CONTINUED

CHEDDAR CORNBREAD WAFFLES

1½ cups buttermilk

1 cup frozen corn kernels, thawed

2 eggs

½ cup melted unsalted butter

2 tablespoons honey

2 cups shredded cheddar cheese

1½ cups cornmeal

1 cup all-purpose flour

⅔ cup granulated sugar

¼ cup thinly sliced scallions, white and light green parts only

1½ teaspoons baking powder

1 teaspoon baking soda

1 teaspoon kosher salt

1 (4-ounce can) diced green chiles, drained (optional)

To make the waffles: In a blender, combine the buttermilk, corn, eggs, melted butter, and honey and blend until smooth.

In a large bowl, combine the cheddar, cornmeal, flour, sugar, scallions, baking powder, baking soda, and salt. Pour in the buttermilk mixture and mix well to combine. Fold in the chiles (if using).

Preheat a waffle iron to medium-hot and lightly coat with nonstick cooking spray.

Spoon about ¾ cup of the batter onto the iron (you'll probably need more batter if you're using a Belgian waffle iron) and cook as you normally would a waffle. Repeat with the remaining batter.

Serve the chili with the waffles alongside.

Put Away and Replay

Store the chili in a sealed container in the fridge for up to 4 days. Reheat in a small pot over medium heat until hot. Reheating leftover waffles isn't recommended, but you can warm them in the toaster, or in a 350°F oven for about 10 minutes, or until lightly browned.

Note from the Matts

You have a few options when it comes to cooking the chili. Make it in a pot on the stove top (as the recipe calls for), then transfer that pot to a 350°F oven with the lid on (make sure your pot is oven-safe). Or brown the meat, add all the ingredients to a slow cooker, and cook for 4 to 6 hours on high heat.

Southern Chicken, Corn, and Bacon Chowder

MAKES 8 SERVINGS

You know they call me Superman, however, did you know I'm also Soup Man? I was an early partner and strategic advisor to iconic soup company The Original Soupman, where I helped open restaurants and get their SoupMobiles on the streets. Their products were healthy, great tasting, and satisfying; exactly what soups should be. If I wasn't downing bowls of their lobster bisque, I'd be reaching for a good, chunky chowder like this recipe here.

8 ounces bacon, chopped

2 pounds boneless, skinless chicken thighs, cut into ½-inch pieces

1 large yellow onion, diced

2 celery hearts, diced

1½ tablespoons kosher salt

1 tablespoon freshly ground black pepper

3 russet potatoes, cubed

3 cups frozen corn

1 tablespoon minced garlic

½ cup unsalted butter

½ cup all-purpose flour

4 cups chicken broth

3 cups evaporated milk

2 cups 2% milk

1 tablespoon Cajun Spice (see page 35)

2 dried bay leaves

¼ cup thinly sliced scallions, white and light green parts only

In a Dutch oven or large pot over medium heat, cook the bacon until browned, about 5 minutes. Add the chicken thighs, onion, celery hearts, salt, and pepper and cook, stirring, for 5 minutes. Add the potatoes, corn, garlic, and butter and stir so the butter melts evenly. Stir in the flour, so it coats the mixture, and cook for 1 minute to cook the flour through. Stir in the chicken broth, evaporated milk, 2% milk, Cajun spice, and bay leaves; turn the heat to medium-high; and bring to a simmer. Then turn the heat to low, cover the pot, and simmer for 1 hour, stirring frequently to keep the soup from scorching on the bottom of the pot. Remove and discard the bay leaves and stir in the scallions.

Ladle the chowder into bowls to serve.

Put Away and Replay
Let the chowder cool completely before storing in an airtight container in the fridge for up to 4 days. Reheat in a small saucepan over low heat for 10 to 15 minutes, or until hot. If the soup seems too thick, add some milk to thin it out.

Note from the Matts

For a smoother texture and deeper corn flavor, puree half of the corn in a food processor before adding to the pot.

Louisiana Shrimp Linguine

MAKES 6 SERVINGS

2 pounds 21/25 shell-off, tail-off shrimp, thawed if frozen

¼ cup extra-virgin olive oil, plus 2 tablespoons

2 tablespoons minced garlic

2 tablespoons Cajun Spice (see page 35), or more if you like heat

1 pound linguine pasta

2 tablespoons kosher salt

¾ cup unsalted butter

1 large yellow onion, diced

½ cup lager beer

½ cup chicken broth

2 tablespoons Worcestershire sauce

2 tablespoons fresh lemon juice

1 tablespoon hot sauce

1 cup chopped scallions, white and light green parts only

Louisiana will always have a special place in my heart. I was an LSU Tiger for three years, and now two of my kids are playing basketball there. I've even been appointed a Special Reserve Deputy by the local St. Martin Parish Sheriff's Office—with a badge and everything. But I'm not the only thing you don't mess with in Louisiana; the food is also pretty hard to beat. There's nothing like a steaming bowl of Cajun-style shrimp to bring back memories.

Pro Move

Add chopped cooked bacon to the mix because . . . it's bacon.

In a large bowl, combine the shrimp, ¼ cup olive oil, garlic, and Cajun spice and toss to coat. Cover the bowl and let marinate in the fridge for 30 minutes.

Fill a very large pot with water and bring to a boil over medium-high heat. Add the pasta and salt and cook according to the package directions, cutting a minute or two off the cook time, so the pasta is still very al dente. Drain and set aside.

In a large Dutch oven or other pot over medium-high heat, warm ¼ cup of the butter and the remaining 2 tablespoons olive oil. Add the onion and cook for 3 minutes, or until translucent. Add the shrimp and its marinade and cook, stirring continuously, for 2 minutes. Stir in the beer, chicken broth, Worcestershire, lemon juice, and hot sauce.

continued ▸

Louisiana Shrimp Linguine

Bring the mixture to a simmer and cook for 2 minutes to let the flavors come together, then stir in the pasta and let it finish cooking in the sauce for another 2 minutes.

Remove the pot from the heat and add the scallions and remaining ½ cup butter. Stir for a minute or so to incorporate the butter with the sauce. Let the pasta sit for 5 minutes to absorb the sauce.

Serve the linguine straight from the pot.

Put Away and Replay
Reheating shrimp is not recommended since they'll likely overcook, but you can store the linguine in a sealed container in the fridge for up to 2 days. Reheat in a microwave on high power for 2 minutes, or until heated through.

Chicken Parmesan Bake

MAKES 8 SERVINGS

This dish is all about the layers for me—you got your pasta, boom. Your chicken, boom. Your sauce, boom. And then you top it all off with cheese, bread crumbs, and butter, instead of having to do every little piece of chicken individually. Boom.

Pro Move

This recipe calls for chicken breasts—and that's all good—but if you hear I'm coming over for dinner, make that boneless chicken thighs.

Preheat the oven to 350°F. Lightly coat a 9 by 13-inch casserole dish with nonstick cooking spray and set aside.

Fill a very large pot with water and bring to a boil over medium-high heat. Add the pasta and cook according to the package directions, cutting a minute or two off the cook time, so the pasta is still very al dente. Drain and set aside.

In a large, deep skillet over medium-high heat, warm the olive oil. Add the chicken, season with the salt and pepper, and cook for 4 minutes, or until browned on all sides. Add the onion and garlic and continue cooking for 2 minutes, or until the onion is translucent. Stir in the marinara sauce and basil, turn the heat to low, and simmer for 5 minutes. Add the pasta and toss to coat. Remove the skillet from the heat and add 2 cups of the mozzarella. Stir gently to combine and then transfer the mixture to the prepared casserole dish.

continued ▶

1 pound rigatoni pasta

½ cup extra-virgin olive oil

2 pounds boneless, skinless chicken breasts, cut into 1-inch cubes

1 tablespoon kosher salt

2 teaspoons freshly ground black pepper

1 yellow onion, diced

2 tablespoons minced garlic

3 cups marinara sauce

2 tablespoons dried basil

4 cups shredded mozzarella cheese

1 cup grated Parmesan cheese

1 cup Italian bread crumbs

½ cup unsalted butter, melted

Chicken Parmesan Bake

CONTINUED

In a medium bowl, stir together the remaining 2 cups mozzarella, the Parmesan, bread crumbs, and melted butter. Spread the cheese mixture evenly over the pasta mixture.

Bake the pasta for 20 minutes, or until the top is deeply golden.

Serve the pasta and chicken hot, straight from the baking dish.

Put Away and Replay
Store the bake in a sealed container in the fridge for up to 3 days. Reheat in a microwave on high power for 2 to 3 minutes, or until hot.

Note from the Matts

You could also cook up some eggplant in the olive oil and use that for a vegetarian option.

Hide-and-Seek Chicken

MAKES 6 SERVINGS

6 bone-in, skin-on chicken thighs, or any cut of chicken you prefer

¼ cup extra-virgin olive oil

2 tablespoons paprika

1 tablespoon kosher salt, plus 2 teaspoons

1 tablespoon freshly ground black pepper, plus 2 teaspoons

3 tablespoons unsalted butter

12 ounces fresh broccoli florets

2 cups chicken broth

1 (12-ounce) can evaporated milk

1¼ cups packaged parboiled white rice

1 cup grated Parmesan cheese

¾ cup sour cream

3 tablespoons dehydrated onion

1 cube chicken bouillon

1½ cups egg noodles

I've always been a fan of making people laugh—putting on all kinds of crazy costumes, playing practical jokes, attempting to hide behind (way-too-small) things. I don't believe in taking life too seriously. But I do believe in showing up and working hard. I'm a lot like this dish. While you're busy *oohing* and *aahing* over the creamy sauce and crunchy noodles, the chicken, rice, and broccoli are doing their dependable thing and filling you up.

Preheat the oven to 400°F. Lightly coat a 9 by 13-inch casserole dish with nonstick cooking spray and set aside.

In a large bowl, gently toss together the chicken thighs, olive oil, paprika, 1 tablespoon salt, and 1 tablespoon pepper. Cover the bowl with plastic wrap and refrigerate for at least 30 minutes, but ideally overnight.

In a large, deep skillet over medium heat, melt the butter. Place the chicken skin-side down in the skillet and brown for 5 minutes. Flip and repeat on the other side. Remove the skillet from the heat and set aside.

In a large bowl, combine the broccoli, chicken broth, evaporated milk, rice, Parmesan, sour cream, dehydrated onion, bouillon cube, remaining 2 teaspoons salt, and remaining 2 teaspoons pepper and mix well. Transfer the mixture to the prepared casserole dish, using a spatula to make sure the rice is evenly spread throughout.

continued ▶

Hide-and-Seek Chicken

Sprinkle the egg noodles on top of the mixture, pushing them down a bit into the liquid; this way they'll get crunchy on top and give the dish some nice texture. Place the chicken on top of the noodles, skin-side up. Cover the dish with aluminum foil.

Bake the casserole for 1 hour 15 minutes; the top should be golden and the edges bubbling. Let the dish sit for 15 minutes to thicken.

Serve the chicken straight from the baking dish.

Put Away and Replay
Store the chicken in a sealed container in the fridge for up to 3 days. Reheat in a microwave on high power for 2 to 3 minutes, or until heated through.

Creamy Spinach and Sausage Skillet Lasagna with Cheesy Garlic Biscuits

MAKES 8 SERVINGS

Remember when I told you that spinach was the only vegetable I'd eat growing up because I thought I was Popeye? Well, not a lot's changed. I may not be such a big boy when it comes to eating *all* my veggies, but I do love tearing into a plate of gooey, cheesy, sausage-y pasta and greens and feeling these muscles getting bigger. You better believe I'm going for seconds.

2 tablespoons extra-virgin olive oil

2 pounds Italian sausage, casings removed

1 large yellow onion, diced

4 cups sliced button, oyster, portobello, or shiitake mushrooms (or any combination)

2 tablespoons minced garlic

⅓ cup unsalted butter

⅓ cup all-purpose flour

2 tablespoons dried basil

1 tablespoon kosher salt

1 tablespoon freshly ground black pepper

4 cups 2% milk

3 cups shredded mozzarella cheese

2 cups ricotta cheese

1 cup grated Parmesan cheese

16 no-boil dried lasagna noodles or boiled noodles, cooked al dente

8 cups fresh or 4 cups frozen baby spinach

Preheat the oven to 350°F. Lightly coat a 9 by 13-inch baking dish with nonstick cooking spray and set aside.

In a large skillet over medium-high heat, warm the olive oil. Add the sausage and cook, breaking it up with the back of a wooden spoon, for about 5 minutes, or until browned. Add the onion and continue cooking for 3 minutes, or until softened and translucent. Add the mushrooms and garlic and cook for 2 minutes more. Stir in the butter so it melts evenly, then stir in the flour, basil, salt, and pepper until well combined. Stir for 2 minutes to cook the flour through. Add the 2% milk and bring the mixture to a simmer, stirring continuously, for 2 to 3 minutes, or until thickened. Remove from the heat.

In a large bowl, stir together the mozzarella, ricotta, and Parmesan.

Spread 1 cup of the sausage-mushroom sauce evenly over the bottom of the prepared baking dish. Top with a single layer of noodles, followed by 2 cups of the cheese mixture, 3 cups of the sauce, and half of the spinach. Repeat with another layer of noodles, 2 cups of the cheese, 3 cups of the sauce, and remaining spinach. Add one more layer of noodles, top with the remaining sauce, and finish with the remaining cheese. Cover the lasagna first with plastic

continued ▶

Creamy Spinach and Sausage Skillet Lasagna with Cheesy Garlic Biscuits

CONTINUED

wrap and then with aluminum foil (to keep it from drying out; the foil protects the plastic wrap in the oven).

Bake the lasagna for 45 minutes. Remove the foil and continue baking for 15 minutes to brown the top of the lasagna. Set aside to cool.

To make the biscuits: Preheat the oven to 400°F. Line a baking sheet with parchment paper and set aside.

In a large bowl, whisk together the buttermilk and ½ cup of the melted butter. Add the flour, cheddar, chives, sugar, baking powder, seasoning salt, 2 teaspoons of the garlic powder, and the pepper. Mix just until incorporated, being careful not to overmix. Drop ¼-cup scoops of the batter onto the prepared baking sheet, spacing them evenly. You should get twelve biscuits.

In a small bowl, stir together the remaining ¼ cup melted butter and remaining 1 teaspoon garlic powder. Brush the top of each biscuit with this garlic-butter.

Bake the biscuits for 18 to 20 minutes, or until golden brown.

Serve the lasagna with the biscuits on the side.

Put Away and Replay
Store the lasagna in a sealed container in the fridge for up to 4 days. Store the biscuits in an airtight container at room temperature for up to 2 days. Reheat the lasagna in a microwave on high power for 2 to 3 minutes, or until hot. Reheat the biscuits in a microwave on high power for 30 seconds.

Note from the Matts

You can add different veggies to the mix, or leave out the meat. To give the biscuits some smokiness, use smoked cheddar.

CHEESY GARLIC BISCUITS

1 cup buttermilk

¾ cup melted unsalted butter

2 cups all-purpose flour

2 cups shredded cheddar cheese

¼ cup dried chives

1 tablespoon granulated sugar

1 tablespoon baking powder

1 tablespoon seasoning salt

3 teaspoons garlic powder

½ teaspoon freshly ground black pepper

M.D.E.

Stewed Green Chile Pork with Corn Griddle Cakes

MAKES 6 SERVINGS

STEWED GREEN CHILE PORK

3 pounds boneless pork butt, cut into 2-inch cubes

2 tablespoons kosher salt

1 tablespoon freshly ground black pepper

¼ cup extra-virgin olive oil

2 yellow onions, thinly sliced

2 tablespoons minced garlic

2 tablespoons minced jalapeño chile (seeded for less heat)

1 (12-ounce) bottle Mexican-style beer

5 cups store-bought tomatillo sauce

½ cup chopped fresh cilantro

CORN GRIDDLE CAKES

3 cups frozen corn kernels, thawed, plus 1 cup if you like more texture

1 cup buttermilk

1 egg

¼ cup unsalted butter, melted, plus more for cooking

My kind of cooking is the kind where you throw a bunch of ingredients into a pot, press a couple buttons, set a timer, and then come back in a little bit to something saucy and delicious. It gives you time to do the things that matter most in life, like play with your kids or get romantic with a lady or gentleman friend.

To prepare the pork: In a large bowl, combine the cubed pork, salt, and pepper and toss to coat. Set aside.

In a Dutch oven or large pot over medium-high heat, warm the olive oil. Add the pork and brown well on all sides, about 8 minutes total. Add the onions, garlic, and jalapeño and continue cooking for 3 minutes, or until the onions and jalapeño have softened. Pour in the beer, cook for 3 minutes more, stir in the tomatillo sauce, and then bring the mixture to a simmer. Cover the pot and turn the heat to low, so the sauce is just barely simmering. Cook, stirring occasionally, for 1 hour, or until the pork is very tender. Remove the lid and continue simmering for 30 minutes, until the pork is very tender and the sauce has reduced. Stir in the cilantro.

To make the griddle cakes: In a food processor, pulse the 3 cups corn, two or three times, just until roughly chopped. Add the buttermilk, egg, melted butter, and honey and pulse another two or three times, until combined.

continued ▶

Stewed Green Chile Pork with Corn Griddle Cakes

CONTINUED

¼ cup honey

1 cup all-purpose flour

¾ cup cornmeal

¼ cup granulated sugar

1 teaspoon baking powder

1 teaspoon kosher salt

½ teaspoon freshly ground black pepper

½ teaspoon baking soda

¼ teaspoon dried thyme

In a medium bowl, whisk together the flour, cornmeal, sugar, baking powder, salt, pepper, baking soda, and thyme. Add the dry mixture to the food processor and pulse four or five times, just until the dry ingredients are incorporated. If using the remaining 1 cup corn, fold in with a spatula just until combined.

In a large nonstick skillet or electric skillet over medium heat, melt 1 teaspoon butter. Ladle about ¼ cup of the batter into the butter and cook for 4 to 5 minutes on each side, until golden brown and cooked through. Repeat with the remaining batter and additional butter as needed.

Serve the pork with the griddle cakes alongside.

Put Away and Replay

Store the pork and griddle cakes in separate sealed containers in the fridge for up to 4 days. Reheat the pork in a small pot over medium-low heat for 12 minutes, or until heated through. Reheat the griddle cakes in a microwave on high power for 1 minute or in a toaster.

Notes from the Matts

If you want to set it and forget it—or to have more room on your stove top while you make the griddle cakes—you can also simmer the pork, covered, in the oven at 350°F. If you want a thicker sauce to serve with the pork, remove 2 cups of the cooking liquid and the onions from the pot and puree in a blender until smooth. Stir the blended onion sauce back into the pot. You could also cook the corn-cake batter in a waffle iron, adding ¼ cup at a time.

Tamale Pie with Avocado Relish

MAKES 8 SERVINGS

This one goes to all my Tex-Mex lovers out there. You got your beef; you got your enchilada sauce; you got your peppers; you got your cornmeal tamale topping; and you got your cheese. I threw in a little avocado salad on the side, too, because it's all about balance.

Pro Move

If you double the amount of American cheese and leave off the tamale topping, you have yourself a chili-queso dip.

To make the tamale pie: Preheat the oven to 350°F. Lightly coat a 9 by 13-inch casserole dish with nonstick cooking spray and set aside.

In a large saucepan over medium-high heat, cook the ground beef, breaking it up with the back of a wooden spoon, for about 5 minutes, or until browned. Add the yellow onion and both bell peppers and cook for 3 minutes, or until the vegetables have softened a bit and the onion is translucent. Drain half the liquid from the pan, then add the tomato paste and cook for 1 minute, or until it begins to brown. Stir in the enchilada sauce, chipotle puree, green chiles, chili powder, 1 tablespoon salt, pepper, cumin, and garlic powder. Turn the heat to low and simmer, stirring occasionally, for 10 minutes. Remove the pan from the heat and add the American cheese. Mix well, then transfer the mixture to the prepared casserole dish.

continued ▶

TAMALE PIE

2 pounds 80/20 ground beef

2 cups diced yellow onion

1 cup seeded and diced green bell pepper

1 cup seeded and diced red bell pepper

1 (6-ounce) can tomato paste

1 (19-ounce) can mild red enchilada sauce

¼ cup chipotles in adobo, pureed

1 (4-ounce) can diced green chiles, drained

2 tablespoons chili powder

1 tablespoon kosher salt, plus ¼ teaspoon

2 teaspoons freshly ground black pepper

1 teaspoon ground cumin

1 teaspoon garlic powder

16 slices American cheese

1¼ cups buttermilk

1 egg

3 tablespoons melted unsalted butter

3 cups shredded pepper Jack cheese

¾ cup all-purpose flour

¾ cup cornmeal

Tamale Pie with Avocado Relish

CONTINUED

In a medium bowl, whisk together the buttermilk, egg, and melted butter. In a large mixing bowl, stir together the pepper Jack, flour, cornmeal, sugar, baking powder, baking soda, and remaining ¼ teaspoon salt. Add the buttermilk mixture to the cheese-cornmeal mixture and stir well to combine. Scoop this mixture in golf ball–size dollops over the meat mixture in the casserole dish. Gently flatten each scoop, so they evenly cover the entire casserole.

Bake the casserole for 45 minutes, until bubbling and golden brown. Let cool.

To make the avocado relish: In medium bowl, stir together the black beans, red onion, tomato, cilantro, lime juice, olive oil, jalapeño, chipotle puree, salt, and pepper. Add the avocado and toss gently to coat, making sure not to mash the avocado.

Serve the tamale pie with the avocado relish alongside.

Put Away and Replay

Store the tamale pie and avocado relish in separate sealed containers in the fridge for up to 3 days. Reheat the tamale pie in a 350°F oven for 25 minutes, or until heated through. You can also microwave on high power for 2 minutes, or until hot.

1 tablespoon granulated sugar

2 teaspoons baking powder

¼ teaspoon baking soda

AVOCADO RELISH

½ cup canned black beans, drained and rinsed

¼ cup diced red onion

¼ cup diced tomato

¼ cup finely chopped fresh cilantro

2 tablespoons fresh lime juice

1 tablespoon extra-virgin olive oil

1 tablespoon minced jalapeño chile (seeded for less heat)

1 tablespoon chipotles in adobo, pureed

½ teaspoon kosher salt

½ teaspoon freshly ground black pepper

2 avocados, diced

Chicken-Fried Steaks with One-Pot Mashed Potatoes and Creamy Black Pepper Gravy

MAKES 6 SERVINGS

ONE-POT MASHED POTATOES

4 pounds russet potatoes, peeled and chopped into ½-inch pieces (see Note)

2 cups heavy cream

1½ cups 2% milk

½ cup buttermilk

2 tablespoons kosher salt

1 tablespoon freshly ground black pepper

½ cup unsalted butter

4 ounces plain cream cheese (you can also use chive cream cheese for additional flavor)

CHICKEN-FRIED STEAKS

6 (5-ounce) beef cube steaks (see Note)

1 teaspoon kosher salt

2½ teaspoons freshly ground black pepper

2½ cups all-purpose flour

1 tablespoon seasoning salt

½ teaspoon cayenne pepper

2 cups buttermilk

3 cups canola oil

This recipe is the best of both worlds—something you could order at a restaurant (which I've been known to do when my trainer isn't with me) but done easy, so you can make it at home during the week. As a flavor fan, I will tell you that grinding up the pepper fresh is going to make all the difference in this gravy.

To make the mashed potatoes: In a large pot over medium-high heat, stir together the potatoes, heavy cream, 2% milk, buttermilk, salt, and black pepper. Bring the mixture to a boil, turn the heat to low, and simmer for 25 minutes, stirring often to keep the milk from scorching. The potatoes should be tender and easily pierced with a knife or fork.

Using a handheld mixer, beat the mixture right in the pot until it's very smooth. Add the butter and cream cheese and beat again until smooth. Let the potatoes stand for 10 minutes to thicken up.

To prepare the steaks: Season each steak on both sides with the kosher salt and ½ teaspoon of the black pepper.

In a shallow dish, using a fork, stir together the flour, seasoning salt, cayenne, and remaining 2 teaspoons black pepper. Place the buttermilk in another shallow dish.

continued ▶

Chicken-Fried Steaks with One-Pot Mashed Potatoes and Creamy Black Pepper Gravy

CONTINUED

One at a time, dredge each steak in the flour mixture, covering both sides and pressing to coat the steak well. Dip the steak into the buttermilk, then back into the flour mixture, pressing again to coat. Lay the dredged steaks between layers of parchment or wax paper as you repeat with the remaining steaks.

In a large, deep skillet over medium-high heat, bring the canola oil to 350°F. Preheat the oven to 200°F, or your oven's warm setting for the finished steaks. Set a wire rack on a baking sheet.

Working with no more than two steaks at a time, add each steak to the oil and fry for about 2 minutes per side, or until golden brown. Transfer the finished steaks to the prepared baking sheet and place in the warm oven. Leave the oven door propped open to vent any steam, so the steaks keep their crisp crust.

To make the gravy: In another large skillet over medium heat, melt the butter. Add the flour and cook, whisking continuously, for 2 to 3 minutes, or until the flour turns bright white and is cooked through. Whisk in the 2% milk, evaporated milk, kosher salt, black pepper, Worcestershire, and hot sauce and continue to cook, whisking constantly, for about 3 minutes, or until the gravy has thickened and come to a boil.

Serve the chicken-fried steaks alongside the mashed potatoes and top with the gravy.

continued ▶

CREAMY BLACK PEPPER GRAVY

⅓ cup unsalted butter (or bacon fat, for additional flavor)

⅓ cup all-purpose flour

2 cups 2% milk

1½ cups evaporated milk

2 teaspoons kosher salt

2 teaspoons coarsely ground black pepper

1 teaspoon Worcestershire sauce

½ teaspoon hot sauce (preferably Tabasco or Crystal)

Chicken-Fried Steaks with One-Pot Mashed Potatoes and Creamy Black Pepper Gravy

CONTINUED

Put Away and Replay

Store the chicken-fried steaks, mashed potatoes, and gravy in separate sealed containers in the fridge for up to 2 days. Reheating the steaks isn't recommended (they'll get tough and lose their crisp crust), so just let them come to room temperature. Reheat the mashed potatoes and gravy in a microwave on high power for 2 minutes, or until hot.

Notes from the Matts

You can peel and chop the potatoes ahead of time and let them sit in cold water in the fridge until you're ready to cook. Make sure to chop them small, which is what gets you that silky smooth mash. For thicker consistency, remove ½ cup of the cooking liquid before mixing. And if you can't find cube steak, use 5-ounce pieces of top round. Place each steak between two pieces of plastic wrap or parchment paper and use a mallet or rolling pin to pound them to about ¼ inch thick.

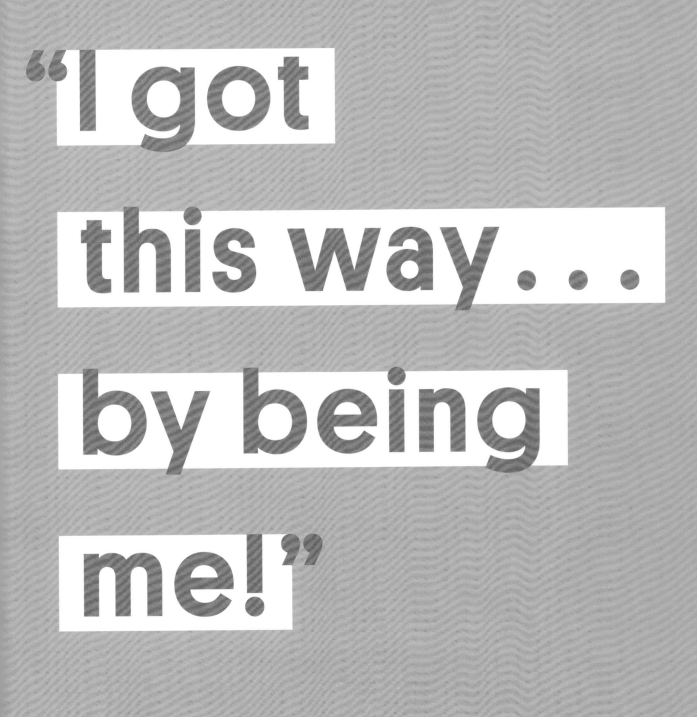

"I got this way . . . by being me!"

Salisbury Steak
with Cheddar-Jack Hash Brown Casserole

MAKES 6 SERVINGS

CHEDDAR-JACK HASH BROWN CASSEROLE

1½ cups evaporated milk

1 cup sour cream

8 ounces plain cream cheese

1 cube chicken bouillon

1 tablespoon kosher salt

1 teaspoon freshly ground black pepper

½ teaspoon garlic powder

¼ teaspoon onion powder

1 (30-ounce) bag frozen hash browns, thawed

1 cup shredded cheddar cheese

1 cup shredded Monterey Jack cheese

½ cup melted unsalted butter

SALISBURY STEAK

2 pounds 80/20 ground beef

2 eggs

¾ cup plain bread crumbs or crushed saltines

¼ cup ketchup

2 tablespoons Worcestershire sauce, plus 1 teaspoon

Back in 2019, I threw my annual Shaq's Fun House Super Bowl party in Atlanta along with Migos, Diplo, Cirque du Soleil, and my man Gronk. We needed food for the event, so I called up a local restaurant and said, "Hello, can we get some waffles and omelets at my party?" And they said, "Sure, Shaq." We even had my favorite order: double hash browns covered in cheese, smothered in grilled onions, and topped with slices of steak. I may not be DJ-ing at your house when you make this but trust me when I tell you that this recipe is a way to bring a little bit of my party to your home.

To make the hash brown casserole: Preheat the oven to 350°F. Lightly coat a 9 by 13-inch casserole dish with nonstick cooking spray and set aside.

In a blender, combine the evaporated milk, sour cream, cream cheese, chicken bouillon cube, salt, pepper, garlic powder, and onion powder and blend until smooth.

In a large bowl, toss together the hash browns, cheddar, Monterey Jack, melted butter, and blended milk mixture and pour into the prepared casserole dish.

Bake the casserole for 30 to 40 minutes, or until bubbling and brown. Let cool.

To make the Salisbury steak: Preheat the oven to 350°F. Lightly coat another 9 by 13-inch casserole dish with nonstick cooking spray and set aside.

continued ▶

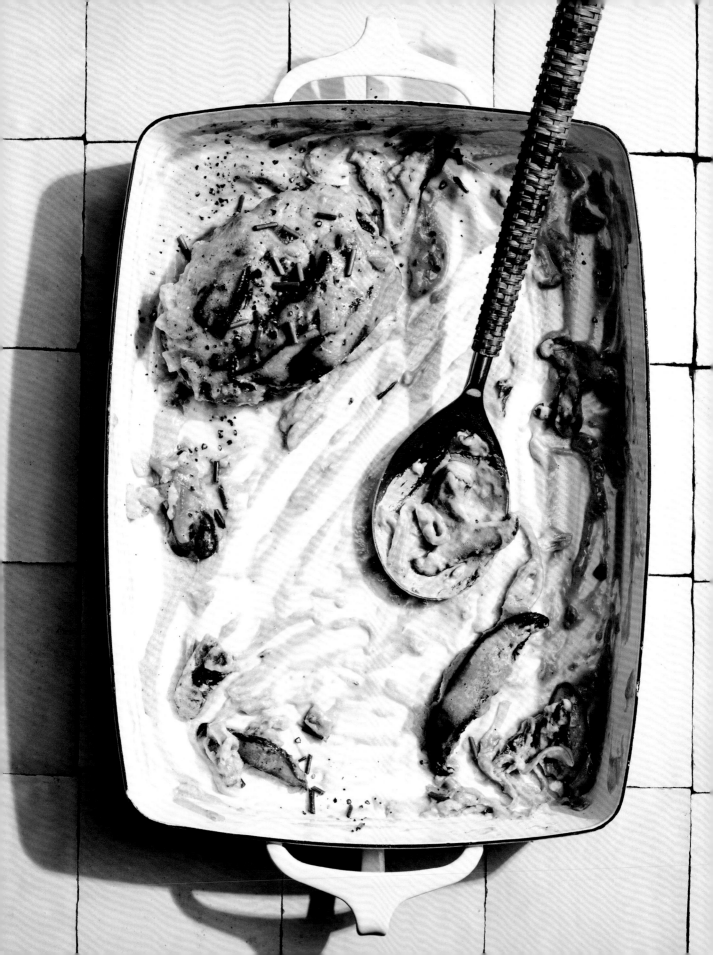

Salisbury Steak with Cheddar-Jack Hash Brown Casserole

In a large bowl, combine the ground beef, eggs, bread crumbs, ketchup, 2 tablespoons Worcestershire, mustard, 1 tablespoon salt, and 1 tablespoon pepper. Mix well to combine. Using your hands, form the mixture into six equal oval-shaped 1½-inch-thick patties.

In a large pan, preferably cast iron, over medium heat, melt ¼ cup of the butter. Add the patties to the pan and cook until browned on both sides, about 3 minutes per side. Transfer the patties to the prepared casserole dish.

Add the onion to the hot pan, turn the heat to medium-high, and cook for 2 minutes, until the onion is translucent and beginning to brown. Add the mushrooms and cook for 1 minute more. Stir in the remaining ¼ cup butter, so it melts evenly, then whisk in the flour until incorporated. Cook for 1 minute, then pour in the beef broth and evaporated milk and add the beef bouillon cube, remaining 1 teaspoon Worcestershire, remaining 1 teaspoon salt, and remaining ½ teaspoon pepper. Stir well to combine and cook the sauce for 3 to 4 minutes, or until thickened.

Pour the sauce over the steaks, then bake for 15 minutes to finish cooking the meat through.

Serve the steaks with the hash brown casserole alongside.

Put Away and Replay
Store the steaks and hash brown casserole in separate sealed containers in the fridge for up to 4 days. Reheat each in a 350°F oven for 20 to 25 minutes, or until hot, or in a microwave on high power for 2 minutes.

Note from the Matts

You can also top the casserole with Creamy Black Pepper Gravy (see page 71) and/or ¼ cup chopped fresh chives.

---

1 tablespoon ground mustard

1 tablespoon kosher salt, plus 1 teaspoon

1 tablespoon freshly ground black pepper, plus ½ teaspoon

½ cup unsalted butter

1 large yellow onion, thinly sliced

3 cups sliced button, oyster, or portobello mushrooms (or any combination)

¼ cup all-purpose flour

2 cups beef broth

1½ cups evaporated milk

1 cube beef bouillon

3

I LOVE PANCAKES

breakfast for dinner

I'm a big breakfast guy. Name a classic morning food; it's on my menu, morning, afternoon, night. I've been known to make myself omelets with a dozen eggs, grab a smoothie if I'm on the road, and dig into a pile of pancakes or waffles more than once a week.

I'm also a creature of habit and I double down when it comes to my meals. It sometimes comes to the point where my friends get mad because we'll go out to the same restaurant year after year, and it's always the same order for me—usually pancakes with grape jelly, and maybe an omelet. I don't care if it's the middle of night; the heart wants what the heart wants.

Buttermilk Oatmeal Muffins
with Blueberry–Almond Milk Smoothies

MAKES 12 MUFFINS AND 4 (7-OUNCE) SMOOTHIES

Smoothies are one of the greatest ways to fuel up in the morning, but sometimes you need another little somethin' to make it feel like a meal. I like these oatmeal muffins because there was once a petition to officially change the name of a certain brand of rolled oats to Shaquille O'atmeal. Oatmeal will never be Frosted Flakes, but that vote of confidence gave me a whole new appreciation for oats!

Pro Move

These muffins are like a canvas for your breakfast art. Add up to ½ cup of other fresh or dried fruits, nuts, chocolate chips, what have you.

Preheat the oven to 350°F. Line a twelve-well muffin tin with paper muffin cups or lightly coat it with nonstick cooking spray and set aside.

In a large bowl, whisk together the flour, oats, baking powder, baking soda, and salt.

In a medium bowl, whisk together the buttermilk, brown sugar, canola oil, egg, and vanilla. Pour the buttermilk mixture into the flour mixture and mix just until incorporated. The batter might be lumpy and that's fine. Pour the batter into the prepared muffin tin, filling each well about three-fourths full.

continued ▶

1½ cups all-purpose flour

¾ cup old-fashioned rolled oats

2 teaspoons baking powder

½ teaspoon baking soda

¼ teaspoon table salt

1 cup buttermilk

½ cup packed light brown sugar

¼ cup canola oil

1 egg

½ teaspoon vanilla extract

PECAN STREUSEL TOPPING

¼ cup chopped pecans

3 tablespoons all-purpose flour

2 tablespoons old-fashioned rolled oats

2 tablespoons packed light brown sugar

½ teaspoon ground cinnamon

1 pinch ground ginger

1 pinch table salt

2 tablespoons cold unsalted butter, cut into small cubes

Buttermilk Oatmeal Muffins with Blueberry–Almond Milk Smoothies

CONTINUED

BLUEBERRY–ALMOND MILK SMOOTHIES

1½ cups unsweetened almond milk

1 cup frozen blueberries

1 banana, peeled

½ cup ice cubes

1 tablespoon peanut butter

1 tablespoon honey

To make the streusel topping: In a medium bowl, stir together the pecans, flour, oats, brown sugar, cinnamon, ginger, and salt. Add the butter and mix with your hands or a fork until the butter is in very small pieces.

Top the batter with the streusel mixture and bake for 23 minutes, or until a toothpick inserted into the center of a muffin comes out clean.

To make the smoothies: While the muffins bake, in a blender, combine the almond milk, blueberries, banana, ice cubes, peanut butter, and honey and blend until completely smooth.

Serve the muffins, warm, accompanied by the smoothies.

Put Away and Replay

Store cooled muffins in a resealable plastic bag or sealed container at room temperature for up to 2 days. Store the smoothies in a jar or other sealed container in the fridge for up to 1 day.

Pull-Apart Buttermilk Biscuits and Sawmill Country Gravy

MAKES 6 SERVINGS

When you've got a bunch of cranky kids wandering into the kitchen in the morning like some kind of zombie invasion and have to get something together fast before they start trying to pull your limbs off, a pan of these biscuits gets the job done every time. Feel free to add some eggs, or top with fried chicken for a Big Chicken–style breakfast sandwich.

To make the biscuits: Preheat the oven to 400°F.

Cut 1¼ cups of the cold butter into ½-inch cubes. In a microwave, melt the remaining ¼ cup butter. Set aside.

In a large bowl, whisk together the flour, baking powder, baking soda, salt, and pepper. Add the cubed butter to the flour and mix with your hands, working the butter between your fingers until most of the pieces are about half their original size, with some larger ones here and there. Add the buttermilk to the bowl and continue to gently combine by hand until the dough just comes together.

Spread the melted butter in a 9½ by 13 by 1-inch jelly-roll pan. Transfer the biscuit dough to the pan and use your hands to spread it out evenly across the whole pan. Dip a knife blade in flour and cut the dough into about 4 by 3-inch rectangles to make twelve biscuits, dipping the knife into the flour after each cut to keep it from sticking to the dough.

Bake the biscuits for 25 minutes, or until golden.

continued ▶

PULL-APART BUTTERMILK BISCUITS

1½ cups cold unsalted butter

3¾ cups all-purpose flour, plus more for the knife

1½ tablespoons baking powder

1 teaspoon baking soda

1 teaspoon table salt

½ teaspoon freshly ground black pepper

1½ cups buttermilk

SAWMILL COUNTRY GRAVY

2 pounds breakfast sausage, casings removed

⅓ cup unsalted butter

⅓ cup all-purpose flour

¼ cup dehydrated onion

3½ cups 2% milk

1½ cups evaporated milk

1 tablespoon freshly ground black pepper

2 teaspoons kosher salt

1 teaspoon hot sauce (preferably Tabasco or Crystal)

Pull-Apart Buttermilk Biscuits and Sawmill Country Gravy

To make the gravy: While the biscuits bake, in a large, deep pan over medium-high heat, cook the sausage, breaking it up with the back of a wooden spoon, for about 8 minutes, or until browned and no longer pink. Add the butter, flour, and dehydrated onion to the sausage and stir to coat evenly. Cook for 2 minutes, enough to just cook the flour, then stir in the 2% milk, evaporated milk, pepper, salt, and hot sauce. Bring the mixture to a simmer, stirring constantly, and cook for 2 to 3 minutes, or until the gravy begins to thicken. Turn the heat to low and simmer for 10 minutes, stirring frequently.

Serve the warm biscuits smothered with the hot gravy.

Put Away and Replay
Store the biscuits and gravy in separate sealed containers in the fridge for up to 2 days. Microwave the biscuits on high power for 1 minute, or until hot, or reheat in a toaster oven. Reheat the gravy on the stove top in a small pot over low heat until warmed through; thin with milk as needed.

Note from the Matts

This recipe goes heavy with the sausage because that's how Shaq rolls, but you can cut the amount in half if you prefer.

Buttermilk Pancakes

MAKES ABOUT 24 PANCAKES

I love pancakes so much they should be called Flap Shaqs.
I'm such a big fan that whenever I go to one of my favorite
restaurants in Las Vegas, Hexx Kitchen, they always have a
jar of grape jelly in the back because, even if it's 10:30 at
night, I'm ordering a stack and they better have some grape
jelly on the side. At home, pancakes are on rotation for
breakfast at least once a week. And while I'm not usually the
one at the stove, my chef Alex taught me how to make the
most perfect, most fluffy pancakes you could want—it's all
about putting a little wrist in the whisk with the follow-
through like a jump shot.

Pro Move

When I cook, I like to use my hands as measuring cups. But to
portion up batter for these, use an ice-cream scoop to make
sure your pancakes come out nice and even.

4 cups all-purpose flour

¾ cup granulated sugar

2 teaspoons table salt

1½ teaspoons baking powder

1½ teaspoons baking soda

2 cups whole milk

1¼ cups buttermilk

4 eggs

½ cup plus 2 tablespoons
melted unsalted butter

In a large bowl, whisk together the flour, sugar, salt, baking powder,
and baking soda. In another large bowl, whisk together the whole
milk, buttermilk, eggs, and melted butter. Pour the milk mixture
into the flour mixture and whisk just until combined, being careful
not to overmix.

Lightly coat a large nonstick pan, griddle, or electric griddle with
nonstick cooking spray. Warm the pan or griddle over medium-high
heat or set the electric griddle to 380°F. Add ¼-cup dollops of
batter to the pan or griddle and cook on one side for 2 to 3 minutes,
or until bubbles form on the top. Flip and cook for 2 minutes more,

continued ▶

Buttermilk Pancakes

until cooked through. Transfer the finished pancakes to a plate. Repeat with the remaining batter.

Pancakes don't keep well, so eat them up the morning (or afternoon or evening) that you make them.

Note from the Matts

We don't think pancakes need a whole lot to be tasty, but here are a few different takes on the classic, in case that's more your speed.

Apple Cheddar Pancakes

Fold 3 cups grated unpeeled Granny Smith apples and 3 cups shredded sharp cheddar cheese into the batter. Cook as directed.

Banana Nut Pancakes

Add 2 teaspoons ground cinnamon to the dry ingredients. Fold 6 medium chopped bananas and 1 cup chopped toasted walnuts into the batter. Cook as directed.

Blueberry Pancakes

Fold 2 cups fresh or frozen blueberries into the batter. Cook as directed.

Chocolate Chip Pancakes

Fold 2 cups semisweet chocolate chips into the batter. Cook as directed.

Grape Jelly Pancakes

Add 2 cups grape jelly (use the squeezable kind for easy measuring) into the batter, folding gently three or four times. You want to leave ribbons of jelly in the pancakes. Cook as directed.

Frosted Flakes–Crusted French Toast with Cinnamon-Whiskey Maple Syrup

MAKES 6 SERVINGS

You can find Frosted Flakes in my pantry pretty much anytime—it's the best cereal ever created and my all-time favorite snack . . . even if Tony the Tiger once said he thought he could dunk on me.

Pro Move ————

If you want to improve your French toast game, knock these out on the Shaq Smokeless 2-in-1 Indoor Electric Grill & Griddle, or use the Shaq Digital Air Fryer on the baking setting (310°F for 13 minutes with no butter).

To make the maple syrup: In a small pot over medium heat, stir together the brown sugar, water, whiskey (if using), orange zest, and cinnamon. Bring to a light simmer and then remove the pot from the heat. Stir to make sure the brown sugar is dissolved. Stir in the maple extract and cover to keep the syrup warm.

To make the French toast: In a large bowl, whisk together the eggs, whole milk, vanilla, and cinnamon. Pour into a shallow baking dish. Put the Frosted Flakes into another shallow baking dish.

continued ▶

CINNAMON-WHISKEY MAPLE SYRUP

3 cups packed light brown sugar

1 cup water

2 tablespoons whiskey (optional)

½ teaspoon grated orange zest

½ teaspoon ground cinnamon

2 teaspoons maple extract

FROSTED FLAKES–CRUSTED FRENCH TOAST

6 eggs

3 cups whole milk

2 teaspoons vanilla extract

2 teaspoons ground cinnamon

6 cups crushed Frosted Flakes cereal

½ cup unsalted butter

12 thick slices white bread (such as Texas Toast)

Frosted Flakes–Crusted French Toast
with Cinnamon-Whiskey Maple Syrup

CONTINUED

In a large nonstick pan or on a griddle over medium heat, or on an electric griddle set to 390°F, melt the butter. Dip each piece of bread into the milk mixture, making sure it's well coated on all sides. Lay the bread in the crushed Frosted Flakes and coat well again. Cook the French toast for 3 to 4 minutes per side, or until golden brown.

Serve the French toast immediately with the warm maple syrup.

Put Away and Replay
Store the French toast and syrup in separate sealed containers in the fridge for up to 2 days. Reheat the French toast in a warm oven for about 10 minutes, or until heated through.

"I've been described as the world's largest eleven-year-old. That's true."

Loaded Potato Waffles

MAKES 16 WAFFLES

1 pound sliced bacon

3 pounds frozen hash browns, thawed

4 cups shredded cheddar cheese

3 eggs

⅓ cup all-purpose flour

⅓ cup sliced scallions, white and light green parts only

¼ cup melted unsalted butter

1½ tablespoons kosher salt

1 tablespoon freshly ground black pepper

2 teaspoons baking powder

Sour cream and chopped fresh chives for serving (optional)

When I started selling my Shaq 2-in-1 Non-stick Rapid Waffle Maker & Skillet, it was because I knew how important it is that people be able to make delicious waffles anywhere, anytime. And now that I know you can make waffles stuffed with bacon, hash browns, cheese, and eggs, I think this might be one of my greatest contributions to the world.

Preheat the oven to 400°F. Line a baking sheet with aluminum foil and place a wire rack on top.

Lay the bacon slices on the prepared rack and bake for 20 minutes, or until the bacon is cooked through and crisp. Let the bacon cool, chop it into pieces, and set aside.

In a large bowl, mix together the hash browns, cheddar, eggs, flour, scallions, melted butter, salt, pepper, baking powder, and bacon.

Preheat a waffle maker to medium heat. Preheat the oven on its lowest setting.

Add about 1 cup of the batter to the waffle maker and cook according to the manufacturer's instructions. Transfer the waffle to a plate and place in the warm oven with the door ajar. Repeat with the remaining batter.

Serve the waffles hot, with sour cream and chives, if you like.

Put Away and Replay
Store cooled waffles in a sealed container in the fridge for up to 2 days. Reheat in a 350°F oven for about 8 minutes, or until crispy and hot.

Shaq Sausage Slam

MAKES 6 SANDWICHES

I'm 7'1", 325, with a 7'4" wingspan and size 22 feet. If you're gonna feed me breakfast, you gotta *feed me breakfast*. This is one of my favorite things to eat in the morning because it's got all your essentials—sausage (a lot of it), eggs, and cheese—piled between two Big Galactus-size pieces of bread.

2 pounds breakfast sausage, casings removed

12 eggs

4 ounces plain cream cheese

¼ cup 2% milk

2 teaspoons kosher salt

1 teaspoon freshly ground black pepper

2 cups shredded cheddar cheese

12 slices bread of your choice, toasted

Preheat the oven to 350°F. Lightly coat a 9½ by 13 by 1-inch jelly-roll pan with nonstick cooking spray and set aside.

In a large, deep pan over medium-high heat, cook the sausage, breaking it up and pressing it with the back of a wooden spoon, for about 8 minutes, or until browned and no longer pink. Remove the pan from the heat and transfer the sausage to a bowl. Set aside.

In a blender, combine the eggs, cream cheese, 2% milk, salt, and pepper and blend until smooth. Pour the egg mixture over the sausage. Add 1 cup of the cheddar and mix well. Pour the mixture into the prepared jelly-roll pan.

Bake the mixture for 30 minutes, or until the eggs are completely set. Sprinkle the remaining 1 cup cheddar over the hot eggs as soon as they come out of the oven. Let them sit for 5 minutes so the cheese melts. Cut the eggs to fit the type of bread you're using.

Sandwich the eggs between two slices of toasted bread and serve immediately.

continued ▶

Shaq Sausage Slam

CONTINUED

Put Away and Replay

Store the eggs in a sealed container in the fridge for up to 2 days. Reheat in a microwave on high power for 1 or 2 minutes, or until hot. Place between two freshly toasted pieces of bread.

Notes from the Matts

If you don't like sausage as much as Shaq, you can cut the amount in half without a problem. We like this on those big ol' oval slices of sourdough, but you could use any kind of sliced bread or bagels.

Bacon and Cheesy Scramble Pockets

MAKES 6 SERVINGS

I'm no stranger to a twelve-egg omelet as a protein boost, but I'd be lying if I said that eggs can't get boring sometimes. So, when I heard that you could take those same eggs, cheese, and bacon; toss in some tots; and bake 'em into a pita, I thought it was the kind of breakfast fitting for a connoisseur like me.

Pro Moves ⁓⁓⁓⁓

You could take the same mixture and cook it into tortillas for breakfast burritos. The cooking technique I use here is the easiest and quickest way to cook nice, crispy bacon. You'll never go back to the skillet.

1 pound sliced bacon

3 cups frozen Tater Tots

12 eggs

1 (12-ounce) can evaporated milk

¼ cup dried chives

1 teaspoon kosher salt

1 teaspoon freshly ground black pepper

¼ cup unsalted butter

2 cups shredded cheddar cheese

6 pita rounds

Preheat the oven to 400°F. Line a baking sheet with aluminum foil and place a wire rack on top.

Lay the bacon slices on the prepared rack. Spread the tots on another baking sheet. Transfer both baking sheets to the oven and bake for 20 minutes, or until the bacon is cooked through and crisp, and the tots are well browned. Let the bacon cool, chop it into pieces, and set aside.

Meanwhile, in a large bowl, whisk together the eggs, evaporated milk, chives, salt, and pepper until smooth. (You can also do this in a blender.)

continued ▶

Bacon and Cheesy Scramble Pockets

CONTINUED

In a large nonstick pan over medium-low heat, melt the butter. Add the egg mixture and cook, stirring frequently, for about 8 minutes, or until the eggs are just slightly firm and still a bit runny. Remove the pan from the heat and add the cheddar, baked tots, and chopped bacon. Stir to combine.

Turn the oven temperature to 350°F.

Cut 2 inches from the top of each pita and open the pitas to form a pocket. Spoon the egg mixture into each pita. Place the filled pitas on a baking sheet and bake for 10 minutes.

Serve the pockets immediately.

Put Away and Replay
Store the eggs in a sealed container in the fridge for up to 2 days. When ready to serve, fill the pitas and microwave on high power for 2 minutes, or until hot.

Turkey Sausage, Vegetable, and Biscuit Breakfast Casserole

MAKES 8 SERVINGS

You could call this a breakfast bread pudding, except I won't call it that because I've never tried bread pudding and I never will. I always say you should never judge a book by its cover, but the name just doesn't sound right. Pudding? With *bread*? Let's just call this what it is: An extra-cheesy, sausage-filled, hide-the-veggies breakfast that fills everyone up in no time.

Preheat the oven to 350°F. Lightly coat a 9 by 13-inch casserole dish with nonstick cooking spray and set aside.

In a large, deep pan over medium-high heat, warm the olive oil. Add the sausage and cook, breaking it up with the back of a wooden spoon, for about 8 minutes, or until browned and no longer pink. Drain most of the liquid from the pan and return the pan to the heat. Add the onion and cook for 2 minutes, or until translucent. Add the mushrooms and cook for 2 minutes more. Remove the pan from the heat and transfer the mixture to a large bowl. Add the spinach and broccoli and stir to combine.

In a large bowl, whisk together the eggs, Monterey Jack, 2% milk, salt, pepper, and hot sauce. Pour the egg mixture over the sausage mixture and mix well.

continued ▶

2 tablespoons extra-virgin olive oil

2 pounds turkey breakfast sausage, casings removed

1 cup diced yellow onion

4 cups sliced mushrooms (any variety)

2 cups packed fresh baby spinach, or 1 cup frozen

2 cups frozen chopped broccoli

12 eggs

3 cups shredded Monterey Jack cheese

2 cups 2% milk

1 tablespoon kosher salt

2 teaspoons freshly ground black pepper

2 teaspoons hot sauce (preferably Tabasco or Crystal)

6 Pull-Apart Buttermilk Biscuits (page 85), or 6 baked biscuits from a can or mix, chopped

Turkey Sausage, Vegetable, and Biscuit Breakfast Casserole

CONTINUED

Scatter the chopped biscuits over the bottom of the prepared casserole dish. Pour the sausage-egg mixture over the top, using a spatula to level the top and distribute any large pieces. Cover the dish with aluminum foil and bake for 1 hour, then remove the foil and bake for 30 minutes more, or until firm to the touch. Let the casserole rest for 10 minutes.

Serve the casserole warm.

Put Away and Replay
Let the casserole cool completely before storing it in a sealed container in the fridge for up to 3 days. Reheat in a microwave on high power for 2 minutes, or until heated through.

Notes from the Matts

Halve the amount of sausage if you're not looking for Shaq-size servings. You can also switch up the vegetables and the cheese depending on what you and your family like. Goat cheese is especially great here.

4

SANDWICHES ALL DAY

'nuff said

Besides Frosted Flakes, sandwiches have always been my number-one performance enhancer. For example, when I was given babysitting duties while my mom and dad were out working, I saw it as leading my first corporation.

My sister Lateefah was my VP of Dishes; my sister Ayesha was the Chief Operating Officer of Bed Making; and my brother Jamal was Director of Leaves. They would report to me as I was sitting on the couch eating bologna sandwiches and watching *General Hospital* (Luke and Laura forever, by the way). When I got older, before games I'd always eat two club sandwiches, some fries, and two pineapple Fantas. But they weren't just any ol' bread-and-meat combos with just two slices of bread and a sad slice of turkey; they were *thammiches*. We're talkin' four pieces of turkey, extra mayo, extra cheese, crisp lettuce, and cold tomatoes piled up really big and then smashed down. Thammich. After games, win or lose, it was more sandwiches. Usually a chicken sandwich, maybe with some macaroni. I've just always been a sandwich guy—for lunch, dinner, and snacks. Needless to say, I know my way around a sandwich, and these recipes are gonna show you the way.

Deviled Egg–Chicken Salad Sandwiches

MAKES 6 SANDWICHES

It's true what's said about deviled eggs—it's not a party until they show up. Any cookout worth going to has a tray of 'em on the table. The same can be said for this chicken salad-mashup sandwich.

Pro Move

Chicken salad, like deviled eggs, can be a personal thing. You have my official blessing to make this sandwich your own. Add roasted pecans or dried fruit, use chicken breasts instead of thighs, roast and shred the chicken instead of boiling it, or go with a different kind of bread. I'm a big fan of the wheat–oat hoagie rolls sold in grocery stores.

In a large pot, combine the chicken, sweet potato, and bouillon cube and cover with 5 cups water. Place the pot over medium-high heat and bring just to a simmer. Turn the heat to low, so the water bubbles only occasionally, and cook for 10 minutes, or until the sweet potato is just beginning to soften. Drain thoroughly and spread the chicken and sweet potato on a baking sheet to cool completely.

Meanwhile, fill a large bowl with ice cubes and water to make an ice bath. Put the eggs in a small pot and add enough cold water to just cover. Bring to a simmer over medium-low heat and cook for 12 minutes. (Alternatively, use the Shaq Egg Maker.) Remove the eggs from the heat, drain, and transfer to the ice bath. When the eggs are cool enough to handle, peel and roughly chop them.

continued ▶

1½ pounds boneless, skinless chicken thighs, cut into ½-inch pieces

1 small sweet potato, cut into ½-inch pieces

1 cube chicken bouillon

6 eggs

1 cup mayonnaise

½ cup finely diced celery

¼ cup thinly sliced scallions, light green parts only

¼ cup finely diced red onion

¼ cup sweet pickle relish

2 tablespoons whole-grain mustard

2 tablespoons rice wine vinegar

1 tablespoon chopped chipotles in adobo

2 teaspoons kosher salt

1 teaspoon freshly ground black pepper

18 Hawaiian rolls

6 lettuce leaves

2 vine-ripened tomatoes, sliced

Deviled Egg–Chicken Salad Sandwiches

In a large bowl, stir together the chopped eggs, mayo, celery, scallions, red onion, relish, mustard, vinegar, chipotles, salt, and pepper. Fold in the cooled chicken and sweet potato and stir to coat evenly. Cover and refrigerate the mixture for 1 hour to set up and thicken.

Separate the Hawaiian rolls into six large, equal pieces, so each "roll" is really three small rolls still joined together. Slice these large rolls horizontally, partially through the middle, so they open like a book. Layer on the lettuce and tomatoes, followed by a few scoops of the chicken salad.

Serve the sandwiches immediately.

Put Away and Replay
Store the chicken salad in a sealed container in the fridge for up to 2 days.

Roasted Mushroom Cheese Steak-ish Sandwiches with Pesto Mayo

MAKES 6 SANDWICHES

Normally my sandwich veggies don't go much further than lettuce and tomato, but it turns out that when you roast some monster portobellos—the Shaqs of the mushroom world—you won't miss the meat on this tasty, filling sandwich.

To make the pesto mayo: In a medium bowl, whisk together the mayo, pesto, and lemon juice. Cover and set aside in the fridge.

Preheat the broiler. Line a baking sheet with aluminum foil and set aside.

Using a metal spoon, scrape out the black undersides of the mushrooms and remove the stems. Place the mushroom caps on the baking sheet, drizzle with ½ cup of the olive oil, and sprinkle with the 1 tablespoon salt and 1 tablespoon black pepper. Broil the mushrooms for 5 minutes per side, or until slightly browned, crisp, and soft. Let the mushrooms cool slightly, then slice them into ¼-inch strips.

In a Dutch oven or large pot over medium-high heat, melt the butter with the remaining ¼ cup olive oil. Add the onions, bell peppers (if using), remaining 2 teaspoons salt, and remaining 1 teaspoon black pepper and stir to combine. Cover the pot and let the onions steam for 5 minutes, then remove the lid and continue cooking until the onions have caramelized, stirring frequently to keep them from burning, about 5 minutes more.

continued ▶

PESTO MAYO

¾ cup mayonnaise

½ cup pesto

2 teaspoons fresh lemon juice

12 portobello mushrooms

¾ cup extra-virgin olive oil

1 tablespoon kosher salt, plus 2 teaspoons

1 tablespoon freshly ground black pepper, plus 1 teaspoon

¼ cup unsalted butter

2 yellow onions, thinly sliced

2 large red or green bell peppers, seeded and thinly sliced (optional)

1 tablespoon Worcestershire sauce

1 teaspoon garlic powder

3 slices provolone cheese

3 slices white American cheese

6 (6-inch) hoagie rolls, split and toasted

Roasted Mushroom Cheese Steak-ish Sandwiches with Pesto Mayo

CONTINUED

Stir the sliced mushrooms, Worcestershire, and garlic powder into the pot and cook for 2 minutes more, or until the mushrooms are hot. Remove the pot from the heat, add the provolone and American cheese, and mix well until the cheeses are melted.

Spread the pesto on both cut sides of the hoagies and stuff them with the mushroom-cheese mixture.

Serve the sandwiches immediately.

Put Away and Replay
Store the mushroom-cheese mixture in a sealed container in the fridge for up to 2 days. Reheat in a 350°F oven for 15 to 20 minutes, or until heated through.

Note from the Matts

For another layer of flavor, grill the mushrooms.

Tuna Cake Sandwiches with Chipotle Remoulade

MAKES 6 SANDWICHES

You say tuna cakes and chipotle remoulade, I say crispy fish in fancy mayo. These are like a Filet-O-Fish in a tuxedo. Once you introduce your mayo to the smoky, spicy adobe sauce from a can of chipotle chiles (the kind you can find in the Latin foods section of your grocery store), it'll be a lifelong romance.

To make the remoulade: In a medium bowl, whisk together the mayo, relish, mustard, scallions, chipotles, lemon juice, and Worcestershire. Cover and set aside in the fridge.

To make the tuna cakes: In a large bowl, stir together the tuna, ½ cup of the bread crumbs, cheddar, mayo, red onion, celery, bell pepper, mustard, lemon juice, chives, parsley, Old Bay, and hot sauce. Form the mixture into six equal-size balls. Place the balls on a plate and refrigerate for 1 hour.

Spread the remaining 3 cups bread crumbs in a shallow bowl or baking dish. Remove the tuna from the fridge, flatten into 4-inch patties, and coat in the bread crumbs.

In a large nonstick pan over medium heat or on an electric griddle set at 370°F, melt the ½ cup butter. Add the tuna patties and cook for 5 minutes per side, or until they are hot all the way through and golden brown on both sides.

continued ▶

CHIPOTLE REMOULADE

1 cup mayonnaise

¼ cup sweet pickle relish

2 tablespoons whole-grain mustard

2 tablespoons thinly sliced scallions, light green parts only

1 tablespoon chopped chipotles in adobo

1 teaspoon fresh lemon juice

1 teaspoon Worcestershire sauce

TUNA CAKES

4 (10-ounce) cans tuna in water, drained

3½ cups plain bread crumbs

2 cups shredded cheddar cheese

½ cup mayonnaise

⅓ cup finely diced red onion

⅓ cup finely diced celery

⅓ cup seeded and finely diced red bell pepper

2 tablespoons whole-grain mustard

2 tablespoons fresh lemon juice

Tuna Cake Sandwiches with Chipotle Remoulade

CONTINUED

1 tablespoon dried chives

1 tablespoon dried parsley

2 teaspoons
Old Bay seasoning

1 teaspoon hot sauce
(preferably Tabasco or Crystal)

½ cup unsalted butter

¼ cup unsalted butter,
at room temperature

6 square ciabatta rolls or
burger buns, split

12 slices tomato

6 lettuce leaves

Preheat the broiler.

Spread the ¼ cup room-temperature butter on the buns, set them buttered-side up on a baking sheet, and broil for 2 to 3 minutes, or until golden.

Spread the remoulade on both cut sides of the buns. Place a tuna cake on each bottom bun, followed by two slices of tomato, a lettuce leaf, and the top bun.

Serve the sandwiches immediately.

Put Away and Replay
Store the tuna patties in a sealed container in the fridge for 1 day. Reheat on a sheet pan in a 300°F oven for about 15 minutes, or until hot.

Note from the Matts

You can substitute crab meat for the tuna.

"I like to say that what keeps me motivated is my MBA—mama, babies, and associates."

The Uncle Jerome

MAKES 6 SANDWICHES

NASHVILLE HOT OIL

1 cup canola oil

2 tablespoons packed
light brown sugar

1 tablespoon cayenne pepper
(use more if you like more
heat)

1 tablespoon smoked paprika

2 teaspoons sweet paprika

2 teaspoons kosher salt

1 teaspoon chili powder

1 teaspoon ground chipotle

1 teaspoon garlic powder

½ teaspoon freshly ground
black pepper

SPICY CHICKEN

¾ cup buttermilk

1½ teaspoons seasoning salt

6 boneless, skinless
chicken thighs

1½ cups all-purpose flour

24 saltine crackers,
finely ground

1½ tablespoons Cajun Spice
(see page 35)

1½ tablespoons freshly ground
black pepper

1½ teaspoons baking powder

Canola oil for frying

I know this is what you came for: a secret recipe from Shaq's Big Chicken. This is one of the original crispy chicken sandwiches that we started serving up because, when it comes to fried chicken, I got your back the way "Uncle" Jerome Crawford, my former security advisor, had mine. These sandwiches are best if you tenderize the chicken overnight—you give it a good, long soak in the seasoned buttermilk, which just takes a minute to get in the fridge. Now, some folks like this super-spicy, Nashville-style. Can I handle that kind of heat? You better believe I won't be making any faces about it. But if you're like me and are not usually into that numb-tongue, sweaty-face thing that happens when you eat spicy food, just skip the Nashville hot oil.

To make the hot oil: In a medium bowl, whisk together the canola oil, brown sugar, cayenne, smoked paprika, sweet paprika, kosher salt, chili powder, ground chipotle, garlic powder, and black pepper. Cover and set aside at room temperature (see Note).

To prepare the chicken: In a small bowl, whisk together the buttermilk and seasoning salt. Place the chicken in a large resealable plastic bag and pour in the seasoned buttermilk. Seal the bag and make sure the chicken is evenly coated. Refrigerate for at least 4 hours, but ideally overnight.

Set a wire rack on a baking sheet.

In a large bowl, whisk together the flour, saltines, Cajun spice, black pepper, and baking powder. Transfer the mixture to a shallow bowl or baking dish.

continued ▶

The Uncle Jerome

CONTINUED

Remove the chicken thighs from the buttermilk, letting the excess drip back into the bag, and place them, one at a time, in the flour mixture, pressing down to coat them evenly on both sides. Set the coated chicken on the prepared rack for 10 minutes. Right before frying, coat the chicken once more in the flour mixture.

Pour about 4 inches of canola oil into a Dutch oven or large pot over medium-high heat, or a deep fryer, and bring to 325°F. Working in batches of two or three chicken thighs, fry the chicken for 5 minutes, or until golden brown and the interior temperature registers 165°F on an instant-read thermometer. If you are not using a deep fryer, you may want to flip the chicken halfway through cooking.

Transfer the fried chicken to a large mixing bowl, being careful not to disturb the crispy breading. Pour the Nashville hot oil over the chicken and toss gently to coat well.

Spread both cut sides of the buns with mayo and place the dressed crispy chicken on each bottom bun, followed by a layer of lettuce, and then the top bun.

Serve the sandwiches immediately.

Put Away and Replay
Store the chicken in a sealed container in the fridge for up to 3 days. Reheat in a 350°F air fryer for about 12 minutes, or in a 350°F oven for about 12 minutes, or until hot.

6 potato buns, split and toasted

¾ cup mayonnaise

3 cups shredded iceberg lettuce

Note from the Matts

To bring out all the flavors of the spicy oil, warm it in a saucepan over super-low heat, to about 115°F, before coating the chicken.

BBQ Pulled Pork–Grilled Cheese Sandwiches

MAKES 6 SANDWICHES

BBQ PULLED PORK

2 pounds boneless pork butt, cut into 2-inch cubes

1¼ cups ketchup

¼ cup packed light brown sugar

2 tablespoons yellow mustard

2 tablespoons apple cider vinegar

2 tablespoons Worcestershire sauce

2 tablespoons molasses

2 tablespoons chopped chipotles in adobo

1½ teaspoons kosher salt

1½ teaspoons freshly ground black pepper

1 teaspoon garlic powder

1 teaspoon onion powder

1 cup red wine vinegar

¼ cup granulated sugar

2 teaspoons kosher salt

1 teaspoon freshly ground black pepper

1 teaspoon pickling spices (optional)

1 red onion, sliced into ¼-inch rings

½ cup unsalted butter, at room temperature

12 slices sourdough bread

12 slices Muenster cheese

12 slices Colby Jack cheese

Back when I was playing for the Cleveland Cavaliers, the folks at *The Onion* thought they were being funny when they ran an article saying I was sidelined for a "pulled pork sandwich" during the second half of a game against the Toronto Raptors. LeBron James was "quoted" saying he could see the injury all over my face. And sure enough, there was a photo of me sitting next to LeBron with sauce all over my face and jersey. As made-up as it was, they only got one thing wrong here—I don't kid around about my pulled pork.

To make the pulled pork: In a slow cooker, combine the pork, ketchup, brown sugar, mustard, apple cider vinegar, Worcestershire, molasses, chipotles, salt, pepper, garlic powder, and onion powder. Set the slow cooker to high, cover, and cook for 5 hours, or until the pork is tender and easily pulls apart. Using two forks, shred the pork in the sauce. Set the slow cooker aside to cool.

In a small saucepan over medium-high heat, stir together the red wine vinegar, granulated sugar, salt, pepper, and pickling spices (if using) and bring to a boil.

Place the red onion in a medium nonreactive bowl and pour the hot vinegar mixture over the top. Let the mixture sit at room temperature for 1 hour, then drain and reserve the pickled onions.

continued ▶

BBQ Pulled Pork–Grilled Cheese Sandwiches

CONTINUED

Set a large nonstick or cast-iron pan over medium-high heat, or set an electric griddle to 350°F. Spread the butter on one side of each of the bread slices. Place six slices in the pan, butter-side down (or as many as will fit at one time). On each piece of bread, layer two slices of each cheese, about ¾ cup of the pulled pork, and pickled onions, as desired. Close the sandwiches with the remaining bread slices, butter-side up, and cook for about 5 minutes per side, or until the pork is hot and the bread is golden brown. Repeat with any remaining ingredients.

Serve the sandwiches immediately.

Put Away and Replay
Store the pulled pork in a sealed container in the fridge for up to 3 days. Reheat in a microwave on high power for about 3 minutes, or until hot. You can also heat it in a 350°F oven for about 25 minutes, or until hot.

Notes from the Matts

Instead of using a slow cooker, make the pulled pork in the oven. Preheat the oven to 325°F, cover the cooking pot with aluminum foil, and cook for 2 to 3 hours. You might have to add some chicken broth if the pork starts to dry out, about 1 cup, or as needed. When pickling the onions, add the optional pickling spices for even more flavor. And when assembling the sandwiches, smear some mayo (instead of butter) on the bread before grilling and it'll caramelize because of its sugar. You could also use any cheese you like here.

Smash Burgers with Jalapeño-Pimiento Cheese

MAKES 6 BURGERS

JALAPEÑO-PIMIENTO CHEESE

1 cup shredded Monterey Jack cheese

½ cup canned pickled jalapeños, drained

¼ cup plain cream cheese, at room temperature

¼ cup mayonnaise

1 teaspoon hot sauce (preferably Tabasco or Crystal)

1 teaspoon Worcestershire sauce

½ teaspoon kosher salt

½ teaspoon freshly ground black pepper

2 pounds 80/20 ground beef

1 tablespoon kosher salt

2 teaspoons freshly ground black pepper

6 sesame-seed burger buns, split

2 vine-ripened tomatoes, sliced (optional)

6 lettuce leaves (optional)

This burger is my Southern-style homage to game-watching nights in front of the TV—an epic griddled smash burger with a pimiento cheese sauce to top it off. *That's barbecue chicken, right there!*

To make the jalapeño cheese: In a medium bowl, thoroughly mix the Jack cheese, jalapeños, cream cheese, mayo, hot sauce, Worcestershire, salt, and pepper. Cover and refrigerate until ready to use.

Set a large cast-iron pan over high heat, or set an electric griddle to 450°F. Divide the beef into six equal balls and season them with the salt and pepper. Place the beef balls in the hot pan and firmly press down with a spatula until they're about ½ inch thick. Cook the burgers for 4 minutes undisturbed, then flip them and place about ¼ cup of the jalapeño cheese on top of each burger. Cover the pan or griddle with a lid and cook for 2 or 3 minutes more, or until the cheese has melted.

Serve the burgers on the buns, with tomatoes and lettuce, if you like.

Put Away and Replay

Store the burger patties in a sealed container in the fridge for up to 3 days. Reheat in a 300°F oven for about 14 minutes, or until hot.

Note from the Matts

You can change up the type of cheese you use in the sauce instead of Monterey Jack—cheddar, goat, whatever you like.

5

SHAQ DIESEL

fuel for when you want things healthy(ish)

They don't call me Dr. Shaq for nothing—it's because I'm who you call when you need to get in shape. Okay, fine, I'm Dr. Shaq because I have a doctoral degree, but still, don't you want to know what a guy who's like a diesel engine eats for fuel?

That's right—no regular unleaded for this man. But I still gotta keep up with my diet and exercise if I don't want to turn my 4.95 (almost 6) pack into a keg. When I started to lose my form, thanks to too many middle-of-the-night thammiches and Oreos, I realized I needed to clean things up. I said to myself, *I wanna take my shirt off on Instagram one more time*. So I started to eat better and make better decisions. Your body is a temple and you have to keep it in shape, but like I tell my kids: You don't have to cut out all the fun stuff, you just have to mix it up. So, sometimes it's lean meats and veggies, and sometimes it's smash burgers and pizza. It'll just be our little secret from my trainer, okay?

Sheet Pan Mushroom Fajitas
with Avocado Salsa and Mixto Tortillas

MAKES 6 SERVINGS

There's a Reddit thread called "Shaq Holding Things," and it's pictures of me holding all kinds of crazy stuff—little kids' heads, a bowl of spaghetti, a seal with my face on it called Shaquille O'Seal. . . . Maybe it's just because I really am good at holding things? I'll tell you one thing: I've never been so happy to have the size hands that I do as when I'm loading them up with some jumbo fajitas. Someone add "Shaq holding his veggies" to the thread.

To make the avocado salsa: In a blender, combine the avocados, salsa verde, cilantro, olive oil, lime juice, kosher salt, and black pepper and blend until smooth. Transfer the salsa to a bowl, cover, and set aside in the fridge.

To make the tortillas: Line a baking sheet with parchment paper.

In a large bowl, whisk together the flour, masa harina, table salt, and baking powder. Drizzle in the vegetable oil and warm water and mix with your hands until the dough is just combined and smooth. (If you'd prefer, use a wooden spoon to get the dough started, but then get your hands in there.) Divide the dough into eighteen equal-size balls and set them on the prepared baking sheet. Loosely cover them with a clean kitchen towel or plastic wrap and let rest in the fridge for 30 minutes.

continued ▶

AVOCADO SALSA

2 avocados, diced

1 (14-ounce) jar salsa verde

½ cup coarsely chopped fresh cilantro

2 tablespoons extra-virgin olive oil

1 tablespoon fresh lime juice

1 teaspoon kosher salt

½ teaspoon freshly ground black pepper

MIXTO TORTILLAS

1¾ cups all-purpose flour, plus more for rolling

1 cup masa harina

1 teaspoon table salt

1 teaspoon baking powder

¼ cup plus 1 tablespoon vegetable oil

1 cup warm water

Sheet Pan Mushroom Fajitas with Avocado Salsa and Mixto Tortillas

CONTINUED

MUSHROOM FAJITA FILLING

¾ cup extra-virgin olive oil

½ cup red wine vinegar

½ cup coarsely chopped
fresh cilantro

¼ cup roughly chopped
chipotles in adobo

1 tablespoon kosher salt

2 teaspoons freshly ground
black pepper

1 teaspoon garlic powder

½ teaspoon ground cumin

12 portobello mushroom caps,
sliced into ¼-inch-wide strips

2 red onions, sliced

1 red bell pepper, seeded
and sliced

1 green bell pepper, seeded
and sliced

1 yellow bell pepper, seeded
and sliced

Using a rolling pin, roll out each piece of dough until it's very thin; about 1⁄16 inch thick. If your dough is a little sticky, sprinkle your work surface with a small amount of flour. Stack the rolled tortillas under a kitchen towel as you work to keep them from drying out.

In a large cast-iron pan over medium-high heat, cook each tortilla for 1 minute per side. They will puff up and brown slightly when they're done. Stack the cooked tortillas under a kitchen towel to keep them warm and moist as you work.

To make the fajita filling: While the tortillas rest, preheat the broiler. Line two baking sheets with aluminum foil and set aside.

In a blender, combine the olive oil, vinegar, cilantro, chipotles, kosher salt, black pepper, garlic powder, and cumin and blend until smooth. Set this dressing aside.

In a large bowl, toss together the mushrooms, red onions, all the bell peppers, and the dressing. Divide the vegetables among the prepared baking sheets and spread them in a single even layer. Broil the vegetables for 5 to 7 minutes, stirring occasionally, or until they are tender and browned. If necessary, rotate the pans, so each pan gets a few minutes directly under the broiler.

Fill the warm tortillas with the vegetables, top with the avocado salsa, and serve immediately.

Put Away and Replay

Store the fajita filling in a sealed container in the fridge for up to 3 days and reheat in a microwave on high power, or under the broiler, for 2 minutes. Store the tortillas in a sealed plastic bag at room temperature for up to 2 days and reheat in a cast-iron pan or on a grill.

Notes from the Matts

These tortillas are a mixture of flour and corn masa, so you get the flavor of corn with the soft texture of flour. You could use shortening or lard in the tortillas instead of the vegetable oil for better flavor. Just be sure not to overcook the tortillas or they will get dry and crunchy. You can parcook them ahead, just about 30 seconds per side, and store in a sealed container in the fridge. Also, you could sauté the fajita mixture or grill the vegetables whole and then slice them.

Shredded Roasted Citrus Chicken and Charred Poblano, Kale, and Cabbage Salad with Honey-Chipotle Vinaigrette

MAKES 6 SERVINGS

ROASTED CITRUS CHICKEN

1 (2½- to 3-pound) chicken

¼ cup melted unsalted butter

2 tablespoons lemon pepper

1 tablespoon kosher salt

2 tablespoons fresh lemon juice

HONEY-CHIPOTLE VINAIGRETTE

⅔ cup red wine vinegar

⅓ cup honey

3 tablespoons chopped chipotles in adobo

1 tablespoon whole-grain mustard

2 teaspoons kosher salt

½ teaspoon freshly ground black pepper

½ teaspoon ground cumin

½ teaspoon garlic powder

½ teaspoon dried oregano

1½ cups canola oil

4 poblano chiles

1 tablespoon olive oil

3 cups thinly shredded green kale

Sometimes, like when I'm trying to drop a few pounds, I know I have to up my salad game. But also, this guy doesn't do rabbit food. So, when I realized that you could basically take all the flavors of a chicken sandwich and put them in a bowl instead of on a bun, I had my fork ready for a workout.

Pro Move

This salad makes a damn fine slaw if you're still looking for some sandwich satisfaction and want vegetable representation.

To prepare the chicken: Preheat the oven to 400°F. Set a wire rack on a baking sheet and set aside.

Brush the outside of the chicken with the melted butter and season with the lemon pepper and salt. Place the chicken breast-side up on the prepared baking sheet and roast for 45 minutes, or until the skin is golden brown, the juices run clear, and the internal temperature registers 165°F on an instant-read thermometer. When the chicken is cool enough to handle, pull off the meat, discarding the bones and skin (or refrigerate or freeze for stock, if you like). Sprinkle the lemon juice over the pulled chicken meat and set aside.

continued ▶

Shredded Roasted Citrus Chicken and Charred Poblano, Kale, and Cabbage Salad with Honey-Chipotle Vinaigrette

CONTINUED

2 cups thinly shredded napa cabbage

2 cups thinly shredded green cabbage

2 cups thinly shredded red cabbage

2 cups cherry tomatoes, halved

3 avocados, diced

1 cup grated Cotija cheese

¾ cup thinly sliced red onion

To make the vinaigrette: While the chicken roasts, in a high-speed blender, combine the vinegar, honey, chipotles, mustard, salt, black pepper, cumin, garlic powder, and oregano and blend until completely smooth. With the blender running, slowly add the canola oil. Cover and refrigerate the vinaigrette for up to 1 week.

Preheat the broiler. Line a baking sheet with aluminum foil and set aside.

Remove the poblanos' stems and seeds, cut the chiles in half, place on the prepared baking sheet, toss with the olive oil, and then turn skin-side up. Broil the poblanos until they are completely charred and black, about 10 minutes, turning them every minute or so. Transfer the chiles to a bowl, cover tightly with plastic wrap, and let sit for 5 minutes. Using your hands or a clean kitchen towel, gently slip off the blackened skins. Slice the poblanos into strips and set aside.

In a large mixing bowl, toss together the kale, napa cabbage, green cabbage, red cabbage, tomatoes, avocados, Cotija, and red onion with 2 cups of the vinaigrette. Add the pulled chicken and charred poblano strips and toss again. Drizzle with more dressing, as desired.

Serve the salad immediately.

Put Away and Replay

Once dressed, the salad is a game-time affair only. Store leftover chicken separately in a sealed container in the fridge for up to 3 days.

Notes from the Matts

If you have some extra time and want even juicier, more flavorful chicken, brine it first. In a large pot over high heat, combine ½ cup salt with ½ cup granulated sugar, 3 dried bay leaves, and 2 tablespoons peppercorns. Add 8 cups water, bring the mixture to a boil, and stir to dissolve the salt and sugar. Remove the pot from the heat and let the brine cool completely. Place the chicken in the cooled brine, cover, and refrigerate for 12 hours. Remove the chicken from the brine and use paper towels to pat it completely dry, then continue as directed. For the slaw, you could char the poblanos over a medium-high flame on a gas-stove burner. Using metal tongs, carefully turn the chiles so they char on all sides (and then proceed with the directions for peeling and slicing). If you're not into the taste of raw onion, soak the slices in cold water for 30 minutes and drain them before throwing them in the salad. If you want an even creamier dressing, add an egg yolk with the other ingredients.

Shrimp and Beer Bake

MAKES 6 SERVINGS

I'm not usually a big fan of beer. For a long time, I couldn't even stand the smell of the stuff because, when I was thirteen, my father caught me sneaking some with my cousins and, let's just say, his punishment was effective. So, don't go thinking that this recipe is some kind of booze soup. No, it's shrimp and andouille sausage and corn and potatoes with all these spices and butter wrapped up in these foil packets and cooked with just a little bit of beer for even more flavor. It's like the best Roc-approved Hot Pocket you could eat.

Pro Move

If it's nice weather, grill these outside and have yourself an enjoyable family cookout. You could also make them in the oven, or better yet, on the Shaq Smokeless 2-in-1 Indoor Electric Grill & Griddle.

1½ pounds 31/40 shrimp, peeled

4 links andouille sausage, sliced into ¼-inch pieces

6 frozen corn coblettes, cut into thirds, or 3 ears fresh corn, cut into 2-inch slices

1 pound red potatoes, diced into ½-inch pieces

¼ cup extra-virgin olive oil

¼ cup dried chives

3 tablespoons Old Bay seasoning

2 tablespoons minced garlic

2 tablespoons dried parsley

6 tablespoons unsalted butter

6 lemon slices

1 (12-ounce) can lager beer

Preheat the oven to 375°F, a charcoal or gas grill to medium-high heat, or an indoor grill to 350°F.

In a large mixing bowl, toss together the shrimp, sausage, corn, potatoes, olive oil, chives, Old Bay, garlic, and parsley until everything is evenly coated.

Cut out twelve 12-inch squares of aluminum foil. Put one foil square on a 10-inch plate and add one-sixth of the shrimp-sausage mixture. Fold up the sides of the foil to make the beginnings of a packet. On top of the shrimp mixture, place 1 tablespoon of the butter, 1 lemon

continued ▶

Shrimp and Beer Bake

CONTINUED

slice, and about ¼ cup of the beer. Cover the ingredients with a second foil square and crimp the edges to make a sealed packet. Carefully transfer the packet to a baking sheet and then repeat with the remaining foil squares and ingredients.

Bake the packets for 45 minutes or grill, inside or outside, for 20 minutes, or until the potatoes are soft when squeezed.

Serve the boil directly from the foil packets, telling your guests to use caution to avoid the steam that will release upon opening.

Put Away and Replay
You can open the packets, transfer the cooked contents to a sealed container, and store in the fridge for up to 2 days. Reheat in a microwave on high power for 1 to 2 minutes, or until hot throughout.

Carolina BBQ Salmon
with Air Fryer Bacon–Brussels Sprouts

MAKES 6 SERVINGS

Salmon is the *real* chicken of the sea—like chicken, it's what I eat when I'm keeping it healthy, and lucky for me, there's all different ways to make it interesting. Take this dish—it's so clutch you could say it's barbecue *salmon*.

Pro Move

You could make these Brussels sprouts in the oven, but I prefer to use my Shaq Digital Air Fryer to get them all golden and crispy with the push of a button. I'm hungry just thinking about it—and that's saying a lot coming from a guy who doesn't always eat all his vegetables.

To prepare the salmon: In a medium bowl, whisk together the mustard, honey, vinegar, mayo, brown sugar, Cajun spice, salt, and black pepper. Place the salmon fillets in a baking dish or resealable plastic bag and pour the mixture over them. Cover and let marinate in the fridge for 1 hour.

Preheat the oven to 400°F. Line a baking sheet with aluminum foil.

Remove the salmon from the marinade and place the fillets skin-side down on the prepared baking sheet. Reserve the marinade.

Bake the salmon for 10 minutes, or until the fillets are firm and the internal temperature reaches 145°F on an instant-read thermometer. Remove the salmon from the oven and turn on the broiler. Brush the reserved marinade on the salmon and broil for 5 minutes, or until the fish is nicely browned. Let the salmon rest for 5 minutes.

continued ▶

CAROLINA BBQ SALMON

½ cup yellow mustard

½ cup honey

¼ cup apple cider vinegar

¼ cup mayonnaise

1 tablespoon packed light brown sugar

1 tablespoon Cajun Spice (see page 35)

1 teaspoon kosher salt

1 teaspoon freshly ground black pepper

6 (6-ounce) fresh salmon fillets, or frozen and thawed

AIR FRYER BACON– BRUSSELS SPROUTS

2 pounds Brussels sprouts, tough stems trimmed and heads quartered

2 tablespoons extra-virgin olive oil

2 teaspoons kosher salt

1 teaspoon freshly ground black pepper

6 slices bacon, chopped into 1-inch pieces

½ cup fresh orange juice

¼ cup honey

2 tablespoons apple cider vinegar

¼ teaspoon red pepper flakes

Carolina BBQ Salmon with Air Fryer Bacon–Brussels Sprouts

CONTINUED

To make the Brussels sprouts: While the fish marinates, in a medium bowl, toss together the Brussels sprouts, olive oil, salt, and pepper. Transfer the mixture to the tray of an air fryer and place the bacon slices on top of the sprouts. Set the air fryer to 360°F and cook the Brussels sprouts for 20 minutes, shaking the basket after 10 minutes so they cook evenly. (Alternatively, you can do this in an oven, roasting the Brussels sprouts on a baking sheet at 400°F for 15 to 20 minutes.)

In a small pot, stir together the orange juice, honey, vinegar, and red pepper flakes. Place the pot over medium-high heat and bring the mixture to a boil. Turn the heat to medium and simmer the sauce for 5 minutes, until it's thickened slightly.

Transfer the cooked Brussels sprouts to a serving bowl and drizzle with the sauce. Toss to coat.

Serve the salmon with the Brussels sprouts alongside.

Put Away and Replay

Store the salmon and Brussels sprouts in separate airtight containers in the fridge for up to 2 days. Bring the salmon to room temperature; reheating it isn't recommended. Reheat the Brussels sprouts in a microwave on high power for 1 to 2 minutes, or until hot.

Turkey Meatballs
and Spaghetti Squash

MAKES 6 SERVINGS

It was one thing to play Big Fella in *Uncle Drew*, but when that BOTB starts happening in real life, I gotta get things in check. That's when I like going for leaner meats, like turkey instead of beef, and spaghetti squash instead of a big bowl of pasta. Which, believe it or not, is just as satisfying as noodles when you're seasoning it like a pro.

To make the meatballs: Preheat the oven to 450°F. Lightly coat a 9 by 13-inch casserole dish with nonstick cooking spray and set aside.

In a large mixing bowl, combine the ground turkey, eggs, bread crumbs, Parmesan, parsley, Worcestershire, salt, black pepper, garlic powder, and onion powder. Using your hands, mix everything thoroughly. Divide the turkey mixture into twelve balls (about ½ cup each) and place the meatballs in the prepared baking dish. Bake the meatballs for about 20 minutes, or until they are nicely browned. Turn the oven temperature to 350°F. Pour the pasta sauce over the meatballs and return the dish to the oven. Bake for another 30 minutes, or until the sauce is bubbling and the internal temperature of the meatballs registers 165°F on an instant-read thermometer.

To make the squash: While the meatballs bake, using a large, sharp knife, halve the squashes lengthwise. Scoop out and discard the seeds. Fill each cavity with water and wrap each squash half entirely with plastic wrap. Microwave two halves at a time, cut-side up and side by side, on high power for 8 to 10 minutes. The squash should

continued ▶

TURKEY MEATBALLS

3 pounds ground turkey

2 eggs

½ cup Italian-seasoned bread crumbs

½ cup grated Parmesan cheese

2 tablespoons dried parsley

1 tablespoon Worcestershire sauce

1 tablespoon kosher salt

2 teaspoons freshly ground black pepper

1 teaspoon garlic powder

1 teaspoon onion powder

2 (24-ounce) jars pasta sauce

SPAGHETTI SQUASH

2 (4-pound) spaghetti squashes

¾ cup extra-virgin olive oil

¾ cup unsalted butter

2 tablespoons minced garlic

2 tablespoons kosher salt

1 tablespoon freshly ground black pepper

1 teaspoon red pepper flakes

Turkey Meatballs and Spaghetti Squash

CONTINUED

be somewhat soft when you squeeze the sides. If it's still firm, microwave for 2 minutes more. Be careful not to overcook the squash or it will be soggy and watery. (A bit of crunch is a good thing here.) Discard the plastic wrap, drain off the water, and let cool to room temperature. Using a fork, shred the squash into spaghetti-like strands and discard the skin.

In a large Dutch oven or other large pot over low heat, stir together the olive oil, butter, garlic, salt, black pepper, and red pepper flakes. Cook for 5 minutes or so, just until the garlic is fragrant and the flavors come together. Add the squash and turn the heat to medium. Toss gently to coat the squash and cook for about 5 minutes, or until it is heated through.

Transfer the spaghetti squash to a serving bowl, top with the meatballs and sauce, and serve immediately.

Put Away and Replay
Store the meatballs and squash in a sealed container in the fridge for up to 3 days. Reheat in a microwave on high power for 2 minutes, or until hot.

Notes from the Matts

Substitute certified gluten-free ground oats for the bread crumbs to make the meatballs gluten-free. You could also sprinkle the squash with toasted bread crumbs or ground oats, which makes for a great side dish without the sauce and meatballs. Last, you can use a stand mixer to mix the meatballs, which allows for a smoother texture.

"Make people laugh and they will remember you."

Breaded Pork Cutlets and Roasted Sweet Potato Salad

MAKES 6 SERVINGS

This meal is what I like to think of as barbecue-lite—instead of a plate of fried chicken and regular white potato salad with all that mayo, you got some juicy, crispy baked pork cutlets and good-for-you sweet potatoes with Popeye the Sailor Man spinach.

To make the roasted sweet potato salad: Preheat the oven to 400°F. Line a baking sheet with aluminum foil and set aside.

In a large bowl, toss together the sweet potato wedges, ¼ cup of the olive oil, 1 tablespoon salt, and 1 teaspoon of the black pepper. Spread the sweet potatoes in a single layer on the prepared baking sheet and roast for 15 to 20 minutes, or until the potatoes are just browned and soft. Let them cool to room temperature.

Meanwhile, fill a large bowl with ice cubes and water to make an ice bath. Put the eggs in a small pot and add enough cold water to just cover. Bring to a simmer over medium-low heat and cook for 12 minutes. (Alternatively, use the Shaq Egg Maker.) Remove the eggs from the heat, drain, and transfer to the ice bath. When the eggs are cool enough to handle, peel and roughly chop them.

In a medium bowl, whisk together the chopped eggs, remaining ¼ cup olive oil, vinegar, sweet pickle relish, whole-grain mustard, honey, tarragon, remaining 2 teaspoons salt, and remaining 1 teaspoon pepper to make a dressing.

In a large bowl, toss together the cooled sweet potatoes, spinach, red onion, roasted red pepper (if using), and the dressing. Set aside.

continued ▶

ROASTED SWEET POTATO SALAD

3 pounds sweet potatoes, peeled and cut into ¼-inch wedges

½ cup extra-virgin olive oil

1 tablespoon kosher salt, plus 2 teaspoons

2 teaspoons freshly ground black pepper

6 eggs

½ cup apple cider vinegar

¼ cup sweet pickle relish

¼ cup whole-grain mustard

2 tablespoons honey

2 teaspoons dried tarragon

4 cups packed fresh baby spinach

1 red onion, thinly sliced

1 cup thinly sliced jarred roasted red bell pepper (optional)

BREADED PORK CUTLETS

6 (1-inch-thick) boneless pork chops

¼ cup Dijon mustard

1½ cups plain bread crumbs

1 cup grated Parmesan cheese

1 tablespoon seasoning salt

2 teaspoons freshly ground black pepper

Shaq Diesel

Breaded Pork Cutlets and Roasted Sweet Potato Salad

CONTINUED

To prepare the pork: Preheat the oven to 400°F. Place a wire rack on a baking sheet and set aside.

Place the pork chops between two sheets of plastic wrap or parchment paper. Using a rolling pin or kitchen mallet, pound the pork to ¼-inch-thick cutlets. Rub the Dijon mustard all over each cutlet. Set aside.

In a shallow baking dish, whisk together the bread crumbs, Parmesan, seasoning salt, and pepper. Press each cutlet into the bread crumbs, then place on the prepared baking sheet.

Bake the cutlets for 20 minutes, flipping them halfway through cooking, or until they have browned on the outside and the internal temperature registers 145°F on an instant-read thermometer. Let rest for 2 minutes.

Serve the warm cutlets with the roasted sweet potato salad.

Put Away and Replay
Store the cutlets and salad in separate sealed containers in the fridge for up to 2 days. Reheat the pork cutlets on a baking sheet in a 350°F oven for 12 to 15 minutes to keep their crispness.

Note from the Matts

For even juicier pork, brine the meat before cooking it. In a large pot, combine 8 cups water with ½ cup kosher salt, ½ cup granulated sugar, 3 dried bay leaves, and 2 tablespoons black peppercorns. Boil the mixture and let it cool completely before submerging the pork in it and refrigerating for 4 hours. Remove the pork from the brine, pat it dry, and continue as directed.

Garlic-Citrus Roasted Pork Tenderloin with Black-Eyed Pea Succotash

MAKES 6 SERVINGS

Sometimes you just want meat and vegetables. That's it. Something simple, a little bit healthy, but still with good flavor. This always delivers.

To prepare the pork: In a large resealable plastic bag, combine the pork, onions, olive oil, orange juice, lemon juice, brown sugar, garlic, 1 tablespoon of the salt, 1 teaspoon of the black pepper, oregano, coriander, and red pepper flakes. Seal the bag and shake gently to make sure the pork is fully coated. Let marinate in the fridge for 4 hours.

Preheat the oven to 375°F.

On a rimmed baking sheet, pour out the marinade, place the pork tenderloins on top, and season with the remaining 1 tablespoon salt and 1 teaspoon pepper. Roast the pork for 40 minutes, or until the internal temperature registers 145°F on an instant-read thermometer. Transfer the tenderloins to a plate, loosely cover with aluminum foil, and let rest.

Carefully transfer the marinade into a small pot over medium-high heat. Bring the mixture to a simmer and let it reduce for 5 to 10 minutes, or until about 1 cup of liquid remains. Remove the pot from the heat and add the cold butter (if using), stirring until the sauce is thickened slightly. Keep warm.

continued ▶

GARLIC-CITRUS ROASTED PORK TENDERLOIN

3 pork tenderloins

2 yellow onions, sliced

½ cup extra-virgin olive oil

Juice of 2 oranges

Juice of 2 lemons

¼ cup packed
light brown sugar

2 tablespoons minced garlic

2 tablespoons kosher salt

2 teaspoons freshly ground
black pepper

1 teaspoon dried oregano

½ teaspoon ground coriander

½ teaspoon red pepper flakes

½ cup cold unsalted butter,
cubed (optional)

BLACK-EYED PEA SUCCOTASH

¼ cup extra-virgin olive oil

1 yellow onion, diced

½ cup seeded and diced
red bell pepper

½ cup seeded and diced
poblano chile

1 tablespoon minced garlic

2 cups frozen corn kernels

Garlic-Citrus Roasted Pork Tenderloin with Black-Eyed Pea Succotash

CONTINUED

2 cups frozen or canned black-eyed peas (drained and rinsed, if canned)

1 tablespoon kosher salt

1 teaspoon freshly ground black pepper

½ teaspoon smoked paprika

1 cup halved cherry tomatoes

½ cup thinly sliced scallions, white and light green parts only

¼ cup unsalted butter

To make the succotash: While the pork roasts, in a large, deep pan over medium-high heat, warm the olive oil. Add the onion, red bell pepper, and poblano and cook for 4 to 5 minutes, or until the onion is translucent. Add the garlic and cook for 1 minute more. Stir in the corn, black-eyed peas, salt, black pepper, and smoked paprika and turn the heat to medium. Cook, uncovered, for 6 to 8 minutes, stirring frequently, or until the juices are simmering.

Remove the pan from the heat and add the tomatoes, scallions, and butter. Mix well until the butter thickens the pan juices. Transfer the succotash to a serving bowl.

Slice the pork, pour the sauce over it, and serve with the succotash alongside, or pass the sauce at the table, if desired.

Put Away and Replay

Store the pork and succotash in separate sealed containers in the fridge for up to 3 days. Reheat in a microwave on high power for 2 minutes, or until hot.

Note from the Matts

For even more flavorful pork, you can brine it first. In a large pot over high heat, combine ½ cup salt, ½ cup granulated sugar, 3 dried bay leaves, and 2 tablespoons peppercorns. Add 8 cups water, bring the mixture to a boil, and stir to dissolve the salt and sugar. Remove the pot from the heat and let the brine cool completely. Place the tenderloins in the cooled brine, cover, and refrigerate for 12 hours. Remove the pork from the brine and use paper towels to pat it completely dry, then continue as directed.

Shredded Pot Roast Tacos with Black Bean–Cilantro Rice

MAKES 6 SERVINGS

Back in the '90s, I was diagnosed with TNS—Taco-Neck Syndrome. I ate so many tacos that my neck was permanently tilted to the side; but in the end, it just may have helped me grab more boards. So, let's just say I have a soft spot for tacos.

To make the pot roast: In a slow cooker, combine the chuck roast, onion, diced tomatoes with juices, both bell peppers, tomato paste, chipotles, masa harina, vinegar, 1 tablespoon of the salt, black pepper, garlic powder, bouillon cube, oregano, and cumin. Cover the slow cooker and cook on high heat for 8 hours, or until the meat is falling apart. (Alternatively, you can do this in a Dutch oven or large pot covered with aluminum foil and cook in a 350°F oven for 2 to 3 hours, or until tender and falling apart.)

Transfer the meat to a cutting board and shred it using two forks. Using a large spoon, skim and discard the fat from the top of the cooking liquid. Return the shredded beef to the pot and add the cilantro and remaining 1 tablespoon salt. Set aside and keep warm.

To make the rice: While the pot roast cooks, preheat the oven to 350°F. Lightly coat a 9 by 13-inch casserole dish with nonstick cooking spray.

Spread the rice in an even layer in the prepared dish. Add the beans in an even layer on top and dot the beans with the butter.

continued ▶

SHREDDED POT ROAST

1 (4-pound) chuck roast

1 large yellow onion, sliced

1 (14.5-ounce) can fire-roasted diced tomatoes with juices

1 large red bell pepper, seeded and sliced

1 large green bell pepper, seeded and sliced

1 (6-ounce) can tomato paste

1 (7-ounce) can chipotles in adobo, chopped

¼ cup masa harina

2 tablespoons red wine vinegar

2 tablespoons kosher salt

1 tablespoon freshly ground black pepper

2 teaspoons garlic powder

1 cube beef bouillon

1 teaspoon dried oregano

½ teaspoon ground cumin

¾ cup chopped fresh cilantro

Shredded Pot Roast Tacos with Black Bean–Cilantro Rice

CONTINUED

BLACK BEAN–CILANTRO RICE

2 cups parboiled white rice

1 (15-ounce) can black beans, drained and rinsed

¼ cup unsalted butter, diced into ½-inch pieces

4 cups chicken broth

1 tablespoon kosher salt

1 teaspoon freshly ground black pepper

1 teaspoon garlic powder

½ teaspoon onion powder

1 cup finely chopped fresh cilantro

18 (6-inch) flour tortillas

¾ cup shredded Monterey Jack cheese

Sliced avocado for topping (optional)

In a medium bowl, whisk together the chicken broth, salt, black pepper, garlic powder, and onion powder and pour the mixture over the rice and beans. Cover tightly with plastic wrap, followed by a layer of aluminum foil. (The foil protects the plastic wrap in the oven.)

Bake the rice for 1 hour 15 minutes, until it is soft. Remove the foil and plastic wrap and stir in the cilantro, fluffing the rice as you mix.

Place the tortillas on a gas range directly over medium heat to char them just slightly, about 1 minute per side. (You can also do this very briefly under the broiler.) Top the tortillas with the shredded meat, Monterey Jack, and avocado, if desired, and serve immediately, with the rice on the side.

Put Away and Replay

Store the beef and rice in separate sealed containers in the fridge for up to 3 days. Microwave each on high power for 2 minutes, or until heated through.

Note from the Matts

You can customize these tacos by adding pickled onions from the BBQ Pulled Pork–Grilled Cheese Sandwiches on page 126, or the avocado salsa and mixto tortillas from the Sheet Pan Mushroom Fajitas on page 137.

6

THE BIG ARISTOTLE

meals for a crowd

My favorite month is March because it's what I like to call "March Chaos." There's a lot of games goin' on, a lot of parties, a lot of people at the house, bettin' money and havin' a good time. It also happens to be my birthday (March 6, if you want to send a card).

In general, between my six kids, my siblings, cousins, nephews, nieces, and all the other people I usually have coming and going all day long, things tend to feel a little bit like a party. The fact is that I pretty much always need food on hand, and I need a lot of it. That's why when I first started learning how to cook, I wanted to make sure I had some good recipes in my back pocket for when I had to feed a whole lot of people, and I needed to do it fast. And while these recipes need to bring the deliciousness, truthfully, it's just as important that I don't have to be messing with the spread all day—serve yourself! That way, no one goes hungry. We *all* have a good time.

Sunday Spaghetti Dinner with Cheesy Garlic Bread

MAKES 8 SERVINGS

If there's one thing I learned from my mama in the kitchen, it's that the secret ingredient is always love. Even if all you know how to make is scrambled eggs, that extra TLC has gotta go in with the salt and pepper. And then there are some dishes where you can really taste when there's something special in the sauce, like in what I call Sunday Spaghetti. It's the kind of meal you can make while talkin', laughin', and kicking back in the kitchen. It fills a whole lot of bellies and it's comforting and delicious—everything you want in a Sunday night dinner.

Pro Move

This is a two-fer—here's an all-purpose marinara sauce *and* a meat sauce you can build from it. The marinara recipe makes enough for this meal plus plenty to go in the freezer for a replay.

To make the marinara sauce: In a Dutch oven or large pot over medium heat, warm the olive oil. Add the onion, garlic, and red pepper flakes and turn the heat to medium-low. Cook, stirring frequently to prevent the garlic from browning, for 8 to 10 minutes, or until the onion is softened. Add the crushed tomatoes, sugar, oregano, basil, kosher salt, and black pepper and turn the heat to medium-high. Bring the sauce to a boil, stirring occasionally, then turn the heat to low. Simmer the sauce, uncovered, for 45 minutes, stirring occasionally. Remove the pot from the heat. You should have about 11 cups.

continued ▶

MARINARA SAUCE

½ cup extra-virgin olive oil

1 large yellow onion, finely diced

10 small garlic cloves, minced

½ teaspoon red pepper flakes

3 (28-ounce) cans crushed tomatoes

¼ cup granulated sugar

2 tablespoons dried oregano

2 tablespoons dried basil

2 tablespoons kosher salt

1 tablespoon freshly ground black pepper

MEAT SAUCE

¼ cup extra-virgin olive oil

5 spicy Italian sausages

1 (3-pound) chuck roast, cut into 2-inch cubes (see Note)

1 tablespoon kosher salt

1 teaspoon finely ground black pepper

1 (6-ounce) can tomato paste

2 cups red wine (anything inexpensive; Burgundy is great)

1 (12-ounce) can evaporated milk

6 cups Marinara Sauce

Sunday Spaghetti Dinner with Cheesy Garlic Bread

CONTINUED

CHEESY GARLIC BREAD

1 cup shredded
Monterey Jack cheese

½ cup grated
Parmesan cheese

½ cup plain cream cheese,
at room temperature

½ cup unsalted butter,
at room temperature

¼ cup shredded
mozzarella cheese

2 tablespoons dried parsley

2 tablespoons dried chives

1 tablespoon garlic powder

2 teaspoons seasoning salt

1 teaspoon freshly ground
black pepper

½ teaspoon red pepper flakes

1 large round sourdough loaf

2 pounds spaghetti

2 tablespoons kosher salt

¼ cup unsalted butter

Grated Parmesan cheese
for serving

To make the meat sauce: In a Dutch oven or large pot over medium-high heat, warm the olive oil. Add the sausages and cook for 3 or 4 minutes per side, or until browned, then transfer them to a plate. Add the chuck roast, salt, and black pepper to the pot and brown on all sides, about 10 minutes total. Add the tomato paste and cook, stirring constantly, for 1 minute. Cut the sausages in half and return them to the pot. Add the wine and simmer for 2 minutes, then add the evaporated milk and marinara sauce. Stir, turn the heat to low, and cover. Cook for 4 to 5 hours, or until the meat is tender enough to easily pull apart. Remove the beef from the pot, shred it with a fork, and return it to the pot.

To make the garlic bread: Preheat the oven to 375°F.

In the bowl of a stand mixer fitted with the paddle attachment, beat together the Monterey Jack, Parmesan, cream cheese, butter, mozzarella, parsley, chives, garlic powder, seasoning salt, black pepper, and red pepper flakes until well combined.

Cut the sourdough loaf in a crosshatch pattern, almost all the way through the loaf but not fully, making squares about 1 inch wide. Stuff the cheese mixture into every cut. Wrap the stuffed loaf in aluminum foil and bake for 30 minutes. Unwrap the loaf and bake for another 15 minutes, until golden brown.

While the garlic bread bakes, fill a very large pot with water and bring to a boil over medium-high heat. Add the pasta and kosher salt and cook, according to the package directions, stirring occasionally. Drain the pasta and add it into the pot with the meat sauce. Turn the heat to medium and simmer the pasta in the sauce to absorb some of the flavor. Stir in the butter.

Serve the pasta sprinkled with Parmesan and pass the cheesy garlic bread alongside.

Put Away and Replay

Store additional sauce in a resealable plastic bag in the freezer for up to 1 month. Thaw at room temperature and then reheat in a saucepan over medium heat until warmed through. Store sauced pasta in a sealed container in the fridge for up to 4 days. Microwave on high power for 2 minutes, or until heated through. Reheat the garlic bread, wrapped in foil, in a 300°F oven for about 15 minutes, or until heated through.

Notes from the Matts

You can use pork butt instead of the beef chuck if you want to keep it all pork. And fresh herbs instead of dried will make your sauce more aromatic.

Brunswick Stew

3½ tablespoons kosher salt

2 tablespoons smoked paprika

1½ tablespoons freshly ground black pepper

3 pounds bone-in, skin-on chicken thighs

2 pounds boneless pork butt, cut into 1-inch cubes

1 large yellow onion, finely diced

10 small garlic cloves, minced

6 cups canola oil

5 cups chicken broth

1 (14.5-ounce) can fire-roasted tomatoes, with juices

1¼ cups ketchup

¼ cup packed light brown sugar

2 tablespoons apple cider vinegar

2 tablespoons Worcestershire sauce

2 tablespoons molasses

2 tablespoons mustard powder

2 teaspoons red pepper flakes

It doesn't get more Southern home-style than this stew, which is basically a big pot of flavor that you can fill up with whatever you want. Traditionally you'd throw in all your leftover smoked meats, so if you've got any pulled pork or grilled chicken lying around, toss it in. You could also add things like okra and black-eyed peas.

Preheat the oven to 375°F.

In a large bowl, whisk together 3 tablespoons of the salt, the smoked paprika, and 1 tablespoon of the black pepper. Add the chicken, pork, half of the onion, and half of the garlic and toss well to coat. Transfer the meat mixture to a Dutch oven or large pot and pour in the canola oil. Cover and bake for 3 hours.

In a large bowl, whisk together the chicken broth, tomatoes with juices, ketchup, brown sugar, vinegar, Worcestershire, molasses, mustard powder, red pepper flakes, garlic powder, and onion powder. Set aside.

Remove the meat from the pot and discard the oil, skin, and bones. Shred the meat and set aside.

In another Dutch oven or large pot over medium-high heat, warm the olive oil. Add the remaining onion and both bell peppers and cook for 4 to 5 minutes, or until the onion is translucent. Add the remaining garlic and cook for 1 minute more. Stir in the reserved

continued ▶

Brunswick Stew

CONTINUED

1 teaspoon garlic powder

1 teaspoon onion powder

¼ cup extra-virgin olive oil

1 large green bell pepper, seeded and finely diced

1 large red bell pepper, seeded and finely diced

2 cups frozen corn

2 cups frozen lima beans

Crusty bread for serving

meat and the chicken broth mixture and bring to a boil. Turn the heat to low, cover, and simmer for 30 minutes. Add the corn and lima beans, replace the lid, and cook for another 15 minutes, or until thick and bubbly.

Serve the stew with crusty bread alongside.

Put Away and Replay

Store the stew in a sealed container in the fridge for up to 3 days. Reheat in a saucepan over medium heat for 15 minutes, or until heated through.

Note from the Matts

Add more types of leftover meats—smoked or not—for better flavor.

Traditional Beef Stew with Sour Cream Dumplings

MAKES 6 SERVINGS

I don't always know my dumplings from my pierogis from my kielbasa—Marcin Gortat could tell you that—but I do know that when it's time for the Big Daddy stew pot to come out, this guy's gonna be satisfied.

Pro Move

If you mash up your dumpling in your bowl and then mix it with the stew, everything gets all thick and creamy.

To make the beef stew: In a large bowl, toss together the beef cubes, flour, kosher salt, and pepper until the beef is evenly coated. Set aside.

In a Dutch oven or large pot over medium-high heat, warm ¼ cup of the olive oil. Add about one-third of the beef and brown on all sides, about 10 minutes. Transfer the browned beef to a plate and repeat with the remaining beef, working in batches and adding the remaining ¼ cup olive oil as necessary.

Turn the heat to medium and add the bacon. Cook for about 4 minutes, or until the bacon is about halfway cooked, scraping the bottom of the pot with a wooden spoon. Add the onions and cook them in the rendered bacon fat for 3 to 4 minutes, or until translucent. Add the butter and continue cooking, stirring frequently to scrape up any bits from the bottom of the pot and brown the onions evenly.

continued ▶

TRADITIONAL BEEF STEW

3 pounds beef chuck, cut into 1-inch cubes

¼ cup all-purpose flour

1 tablespoon kosher salt

2 teaspoons freshly ground black pepper

½ cup extra-virgin olive oil

8 ounces bacon, cut into 1-inch pieces

2 yellow onions, sliced

¼ cup unsalted butter

1 cup cooking sherry

1 cup red wine (anything inexpensive; Burgundy is great)

6 cups beef broth

2 tablespoons Worcestershire sauce

2 cubes beef bouillon

2 teaspoons garlic powder

3 dried bay leaves

1 teaspoon dried thyme

3 large carrots, peeled and diced

3 russet potatoes, peeled and diced

Traditional Beef Stew with Sour Cream Dumplings

CONTINUED

When the onions are well-browned, about 10 minutes, add the sherry and red wine and turn the heat to high. Bring the onion mixture to a boil and continue cooking for about 6 minutes, or until the liquid reduces by half. Stir in the browned beef, beef broth, Worcestershire, bouillon cubes, garlic powder, bay leaves, and thyme. Bring the stew back to a boil and then turn the heat to low. Cover and simmer for 1½ hours, or until the beef is very tender. Remove the bay leaves and stir in the carrots and potatoes. Re-cover the pot and cook for 15 minutes more.

To make the dumplings: While the stew cooks, in a large bowl, whisk together the flour, chives, baking powder, table salt, and pepper. In a medium bowl, whisk together the sour cream, whole milk, and mustard. Pour the sour cream mixture over the flour mixture and mix thoroughly until it is soft and scoopable.

Using a ¼-cup measure or a large spoon, scoop the dumpling mixture and place about twelve balls on top of the stew. Cover and cook over low heat for 20 minutes more, or until the dumplings are firm.

Garnish the stew and dumplings with parsley and serve immediately.

Put Away and Replay
Store the stew in a sealed container in the fridge for up to 4 days. Microwave on high power for 2 minutes, or until heated through.

Note from the Matts

This recipe uses French onion soup as an inspiration. If you want to try something different, melt Gruyère cheese over the top. Just spoon the stew into individual heatproof bowls, sprinkle with the cheese, and place under a broiler until the cheese is golden and bubbly.

SOUR CREAM DUMPLINGS

1½ cups all-purpose flour

2 tablespoons dried chives

1 tablespoon baking powder

1 teaspoon table salt

1 teaspoon freshly ground black pepper

¾ cup sour cream

¾ cup whole milk

2 tablespoons whole-grain mustard

Chopped fresh parsley for garnish

Smart Cooker Spicy Jambalaya with Andouille Meatballs

MAKES 8 SERVINGS

I got hooked on jambalaya when I played college ball at LSU. I got my recipe for jambalaya from Dane Huvall, my best friend from college, and his mom, Evelyn—or "Poonie," as I call her—my second mom. I spent some time living in Cecilia, Louisiana, because of them. They gave me a hard time about wanting to learn how to make jambalaya; but it was worth it for a taste of Louisiana anytime I want. What makes cooking this dish especially easy is making it in my Shaq Smart IQ Induction Cooking Station. We're talking a press of a button and that's it.

To make the meatballs: Preheat the oven to 400°F. Line a baking sheet with aluminum foil and set aside.

In a large bowl, thoroughly combine the ground pork, sugar, dehydrated onion, garlic, mustard powder, red pepper flakes, salt, black pepper, cayenne, and thyme. Using a tablespoon, form the pork mixture into balls and evenly space them on the prepared baking sheet. Bake the meatballs for 10 minutes, or until nicely browned.

Set a smart cooker to the sauté setting, then add olive oil and the meatballs and their fat and stir to rewarm the fat. Then add the celery hearts, yellow onion, bell pepper, and garlic. Cook until the onion is translucent, about 5 minutes. Add the chicken broth, shrimp, chicken, rice, bay leaves, smoked paprika, salt,

continued ▶

ANDOUILLE MEATBALLS

1 pound ground pork

2 tablespoons granulated sugar

2 tablespoons dehydrated onion

1 tablespoon minced garlic

1 tablespoon mustard powder

1 tablespoon red pepper flakes

1 tablespoon kosher salt

2 teaspoons freshly ground black pepper

2 teaspoons cayenne pepper

1 teaspoon dried thyme

2 tablespoons extra-virgin olive oil

2 celery hearts, diced

1 large yellow onion, diced

1 large green bell pepper, seeded and diced

1 tablespoon minced garlic

3½ cups chicken broth

1 pound 31/40 whole shelled shrimp

1 pound boneless, skinless chicken thighs, diced into ½-inch pieces

2 cups parboiled white rice

Smart Cooker Spicy Jambalaya with Andouille Meatballs

2 dried bay leaves

1 tablespoon smoked paprika

1 tablespoon kosher salt

2 teaspoons freshly ground black pepper

1 teaspoon sweet paprika

½ teaspoon cayenne pepper

½ teaspoon dried oregano

½ teaspoon dried thyme

½ teaspoon chili powder

½ cup chopped scallions, white and light green parts only

black pepper, sweet paprika, cayenne, oregano, thyme, and chili powder and stir to combine. Cover the smart cooker, turn on the braise function at 250°F, and cook for 40 minutes. Stir in the scallions.

Serve the jambalaya immediately.

Put Away and Replay

Store the jambalaya in a sealed container in the fridge for up to 3 days. Reheat in a sauté pan over medium heat with a bit of chicken broth and butter for about 15 minutes, or until hot.

Notes from the Matts

You can use precooked andouille sausage if you don't want to make the meatballs. You can also make this dish on the stove top in a Dutch oven or other large pot. Just turn the heat to low and cook, covered, for 40 minutes, or until the rice has absorbed all the liquid.

Oven-Roasted Honey-Mustard Turkey Breast with Black Pepper Sourdough Stuffing

MAKES 6 SERVINGS

I've always said that Thanksgiving should be a weekly holiday. Between giving thanks for all the blessings, being with family, and the food, I don't see any reason we should have to wait around all year. With this recipe, you can make every day Turkey Day. And the best part? You can turn the leftovers into some Superman-level sandwiches.

To prepare the turkey breast: In a very large bowl, whisk together the warm water, sugar, ½ cup salt, 3 tablespoons pepper, thyme, oregano, and bay leaves. Add the turkey breast, cover, and refrigerate overnight.

Preheat the oven to 350°F. Set a wire rack on a rimmed baking sheet and set aside.

In a medium bowl, whisk together the mustard, honey, mayo, remaining 1 teaspoon salt, and remaining ½ teaspoon pepper. Remove the turkey from the brine and pat dry. Using your hands, coat the entire turkey breast with the honey-mustard mixture.

Set the coated turkey breast on the prepared rack and roast in the oven for 50 minutes, or until the internal temperature reaches 155°F on an instant-read thermometer. Loosely tent the turkey with aluminum foil and let rest at room temperature for 30 minutes to finish cooking.

To make the stuffing: While the turkey is in the oven, coat a 9 by 13-inch casserole dish with ¼ cup of the butter and set aside.

OVEN-ROASTED HONEY-MUSTARD TURKEY BREAST

8 cups warm water

½ cup granulated sugar

½ cup kosher salt, plus 1 teaspoon

3 tablespoons freshly ground black pepper, plus ½ teaspoon

2 teaspoons dried thyme

2 teaspoons dried oregano

4 dried bay leaves

1 (3-pound) skin-on, boneless turkey breast

¼ cup Dijon mustard

¼ cup honey

3 tablespoons mayonnaise

BLACK PEPPER SOURDOUGH STUFFING

¾ cup unsalted butter, at room temperature

¼ cup extra-virgin olive oil

1 pound breakfast sausage, casings removed

1 large yellow onion, finely diced

2 celery hearts, finely diced

continued ▶

Oven-Roasted Honey-Mustard Turkey Breast with Black Pepper Sourdough Stuffing

CONTINUED

In a Dutch oven or large pot over medium-high heat, warm the olive oil. Add the sausage and cook, stirring, for about 8 minutes, or until browned. Add the onion and celery hearts and turn the heat to medium. Cook for 4 to 5 minutes, or until the onion is translucent. Add the apples, remaining ½ cup butter, sage, 1 tablespoon of the salt, and 1 tablespoon of the pepper and cook for 3 minutes, stirring frequently. Remove the pot from the heat and transfer the mixture to a baking sheet to cool for 5 minutes.

In a large bowl, whisk together the eggs, chicken broth, remaining 1 tablespoon salt, and remaining 1 tablespoon pepper. Add the cooked sausage mixture and the bread cubes and mix gently by hand, just until the bread has softened and absorbed the egg mixture. Transfer the stuffing to the prepared casserole dish and cover tightly with a layer of plastic wrap, followed by a layer of aluminum foil. (Don't skip this part; the plastic wrap ensures that the stuffing rises and stays moist. The foil protects the plastic wrap in the oven.) Bake for 1 hour, remove the foil and plastic wrap, and bake for another 25 minutes to brown the top and the edges. Let the stuffing rest for 5 minutes.

Serve the turkey breast with the stuffing alongside.

Put Away and Replay
Store the turkey and stuffing in separate sealed containers in the fridge for up to 4 days. Microwave each on high power for 2 minutes, or until heated through.

Note from the Matts

If you prefer to use white and dark meat, you can roast a whole turkey instead. It'll take longer—about 15 minutes per pound.

3 large Granny Smith apples, peeled and diced

2 tablespoons dried sage

2 tablespoons kosher salt

2 tablespoons freshly ground black pepper

12 eggs

3 cups chicken broth

2 loaves sourdough, cut into 1-inch cubes

Cheddar-Crust Chicken Potpie

MAKES 8 SERVINGS

CHEDDAR CRUST

1½ cups shredded
cheddar cheese

1¼ cups all-purpose flour

⅓ cup cold unsalted butter,
cut into ½-inch pieces

⅓ cup granulated sugar

3 tablespoons dried chives

2½ teaspoons seasoning salt

2 teaspoons freshly ground
black pepper

1 egg yolk

POTPIE FILLING

¼ cup extra-virgin olive oil

2 pounds boneless, skinless
chicken thighs, cut into
¾-inch pieces

8 ounces button mushrooms,
diced

12 ounces red potatoes,
left unpeeled and diced

2 celery hearts, diced

1 yellow onion, diced

1 large carrot, peeled
and diced

1 teaspoon minced garlic

½ cup unsalted butter

½ cup all-purpose flour

2 tablespoons dried chives

I'm not usually a fan of foods that sound like weird combinations of things. (Banana pudding + ice cream? I'll pass, thank you very much. I love banana pudding and I love ice cream, but not together.) But chicken + pie is an exception I'll make, especially if that flaky crust gets the extra-cheese treatment.

To make the crust: In a large bowl, using a fork, mix together the cheddar, flour, butter, sugar, chives, seasoning salt, pepper, and egg yolk. Using your hands or the fork, work the butter into very small pieces, about the size of a pea. The dough should have a sandy, streusel-like texture. Set aside in a sealed container in the fridge.

Preheat the oven to 350°F. Lightly coat a 9 by 13-inch casserole dish with nonstick cooking spray and line a baking sheet with aluminum foil. Set both aside.

To make the filling: In a large, deep sauté pan over medium-high heat, warm the olive oil. Add the chicken and cook for about 5 minutes, or until browned. Turn the heat to medium and add the mushrooms, potatoes, celery hearts, onion, and carrot. Cook until the onion is translucent, about 2 minutes. Add the garlic and cook for 2 minutes more. Stir in the butter and let it melt, then add the flour, chives, parsley, pepper, kosher salt, and thyme. Cook for 2 minutes, or until everything is evenly coated in the flour and chicken drippings. Stir in the chicken broth, evaporated milk, bouillon cubes, and Worcestershire and cook for 2 to 3 minutes, or until the sauce has thickened slightly. Remove the pan from the heat and stir in the peas.

continued ▶

Cheddar-Crust Chicken Potpie

CONTINUED

2 tablespoons dried parsley

1½ tablespoons freshly ground black pepper

1 tablespoon kosher salt

1 teaspoon dried thyme

2 cups chicken broth

1 (12-ounce) can evaporated milk

2 cubes chicken bouillon

2 teaspoons Worcestershire sauce

1 cup frozen peas

Transfer the filling to the prepared casserole dish and evenly crumble the crust mixture over it. Set the casserole dish on the prepared baking sheet and bake, uncovered, for 45 minutes, or until bubbly and golden on top. Let the potpie sit for 10 minutes.

Serve the potpie hot from the casserole dish.

Put Away and Replay

Store the potpie, wrapped in plastic, in the fridge for up to 2 days. Reheat, uncovered, in a 300°F oven for about 25 minutes, or until the topping is crisp and the filling is heated through.

Note from the Matts

This approach to the cheddar crust makes it easy for people who don't want to roll out pie dough. But you can use a more traditional piecrust, if you prefer it.

Buffalo Chicken Legs and Blue Cheese Tater Tot Casserole

MAKES 6 SERVINGS

I don't know why, but people are always trying to get me to eat spicy things in all these crazy challenges. Maybe because they think they can get me to crack and make a face. But they should know I'm tougher than that. Recently, Gronk and I competed in a chicken wings–eating contest as part of our virtual Party with a Purpose to raise money for the NAACP and the Boys & Girls Clubs of America. They came at me with some ghost reaper something-or-other pepper sauce. I got a nice little sweat on. And I might have been pouring a gallon of milk in my mouth and my eyes might have turned red, but guess what? No face. Even though I know how to keep it cool at all times that doesn't mean I want my chicken to be face-melting spicy. These Buffalo legs are what the good Lord intended chicken to be.

Pro Move

Use wings instead of legs and challenge your friends to see who can eat the most. Count me in.

To make the casserole: Preheat the oven to 350°F. Lightly coat a 9 by 13-inch casserole dish with nonstick cooking spray and set aside.

In a large skillet over medium heat, cook the bacon for about 8 minutes, or until browned and crispy. Transfer the bacon to a plate and discard the fat.

continued ▶

BLUE CHEESE TATER TOT CASSEROLE

8 slices bacon, cut into 1-inch pieces

1 (12-ounce) can evaporated milk

1 cup sour cream

¼ cup thinly sliced scallions, white and light green parts only

1 tablespoon dried chives

1 tablespoon dried parsley

1 tablespoon Worcestershire sauce

2 teaspoons hot sauce (preferably Tabasco or Crystal)

1 teaspoon garlic powder

1 teaspoon kosher salt

1 teaspoon freshly ground black pepper

1 (32-ounce) bag frozen Tater Tots

2¼ cups crumbled blue cheese

1 cup shredded Monterey Jack cheese

Buffalo Chicken Legs and Blue Cheese Tater Tot Casserole

CONTINUED

In a large bowl, whisk together the evaporated milk, sour cream, scallions, chives, parsley, Worcestershire, hot sauce, garlic powder, salt, and pepper. Add the tots, 2 cups of the blue cheese, Monterey Jack, and bacon and toss well to coat. Transfer the mixture to the prepared dish, sprinkle with the remaining ¼ cup blue cheese, and cover with aluminum foil. Bake the casserole for 1 hour, remove the foil, and bake for another 20 minutes to brown the top. Tent with foil to keep warm.

To prepare the chicken legs: If cooking separately from the casserole, preheat the oven to 375°F. Otherwise, keep the oven at 350°F. Set a wire rack on a rimmed baking sheet and set aside.

In a large bowl, whisk together the mayo and ranch dressing mix. Toss the chicken legs in the ranch mayo and transfer to the prepared rack. Bake the chicken for 40 minutes if cooking at 375°F, or 1 hour 30 minutes if cooking at 350°F, or until the internal temperature registers 165°F on an instant-read thermometer.

Meanwhile, in a small saucepan over low heat, melt together the hot sauce, butter, and honey. Transfer the warm sauce to a large bowl, add the cooked chicken legs, and toss to coat.

Serve the chicken immediately with the casserole alongside.

Put Away and Replay
Store the chicken and casserole in separate sealed containers in the fridge for up to 3 days. Reheat in a 350°F oven for about 25 minutes, or until heated through.

BUFFALO CHICKEN LEGS

½ cup mayonnaise

1 (1.5-ounce) packet ranch dressing mix

18 chicken legs

1 cup Frank's RedHot sauce

¼ cup unsalted butter

2 tablespoons honey

BBQ St. Louis Ribs
with Creamy Blue Cheese Slaw

BBQ ST. LOUIS RIBS

¼ cup paprika

¼ cup packed
light brown sugar

¼ cup kosher salt

2 tablespoons chili powder

1 tablespoon garlic powder

1 tablespoon ground mustard

1 tablespoon freshly ground
black pepper

2 teaspoons dried thyme

2 teaspoons onion powder

2 teaspoons cayenne pepper

1 teaspoon ground cumin

3 racks ribs, 3 to 4 pounds
each (see Note)

¼ cup yellow mustard

2 (12-ounce) cans lager beer

1 pound unsalted butter

2 cups honey

1 (7-ounce) can chipotles in
adobo, pureed

Ribs, in general, are a way to my heart, but any time I have St. Louis ribs, in particular, they take me back to the time I challenged baseball legend, then–St. Louis Cardinal, and all-around great guy Albert Pujols to a homerun derby for my show *Shaq Vs*. After all, they didn't call me Shaquie Robinson for nothing back when I was a T-ball all-star. Albert got a few more on me (just a few), but then again, the guy hits a baseball the same way I dunk and eat ribs—with total destruction.

To prepare the ribs: Place a wire rack on a rimmed baking sheet. (You may need two baking sheets for this.) Set aside.

In a medium bowl, whisk together the paprika, brown sugar, kosher salt, chili powder, garlic powder, ground mustard, black pepper, thyme, onion powder, cayenne, and cumin.

If the butcher hasn't already done so, use a sharp knife to carefully remove the membrane from the back of the ribs. Rub the yellow mustard all over the ribs and then coat with the spice mixture. Set the seasoned ribs on the baking sheet(s). (If desired, cover the ribs with aluminum foil and refrigerate overnight. Remove the foil before proceeding.)

Preheat the oven to 325°F.

continued ▶

BBQ St. Louis Ribs with Creamy Blue Cheese Slaw

CREAMY BLUE CHEESE SLAW

8 ounces bacon, cut into
1-inch pieces

1½ cups mayonnaise

1 cup crumbled blue cheese

¼ cup dried chives

¼ cup red wine vinegar

¼ cup granulated sugar

2 tablespoons whole-grain
mustard

2 teaspoons celery salt

1 teaspoon freshly ground
black pepper

½ teaspoon onion powder

½ teaspoon garlic powder

½ small head green cabbage,
thinly sliced

1 large carrot, peeled and
shredded

1 large Granny Smith apple,
shredded

½ red onion, thinly sliced
(see Note)

Pour the beer into the baking sheet(s). Wrap the entire baking sheet and ribs with a layer of plastic wrap, followed by a layer of foil. (The foil protects the plastic wrap in the oven.) Bake the ribs for 2½ hours, or until the bones are visible and the meat is fork-tender. To check for doneness, being careful to avoid the steam, peel back the foil and plastic wrap and, using the tines of a fork, test to see if the meat pulls apart. If it does not, rewrap and continue to cook, testing for doneness at 10-minute intervals.

In a small pot over medium heat, melt together the butter, honey, and chipotle puree. Set aside until the ribs are done cooking.

To make the slaw: While the ribs cook, in a large pan over medium heat, cook the bacon for about 8 minutes, or until it's browned and crispy. Using tongs or a slotted spoon, transfer the cooked bacon to a plate and reserve the bacon fat.

In a large bowl, whisk together the mayo, blue cheese, chives, vinegar, granulated sugar, whole-grain mustard, celery salt, black pepper, onion powder, garlic powder, and reserved bacon fat. Add the cabbage, carrot, apple, and red onion and toss thoroughly to coat. Top with the crispy bacon.

When the ribs are done cooking, spoon the melted butter mixture all over them. Turn on the broiler and return the ribs to the oven for 4 to 5 minutes, or until they are nicely glazed and browned. Let rest for 5 minutes.

Cut the ribs into two-bone pieces and serve with the slaw alongside.

continued ▶

BBQ St. Louis Ribs with Creamy Blue Cheese Slaw

CONTINUED

Put Away and Replay

Store the ribs and slaw in separate sealed containers in the fridge for up to 3 days. To reheat the ribs, wrap them in foil and warm in a 350°F oven for 20 minutes, or until heated through. You can also reheat them in a 350°F air fryer for 15 minutes.

Notes from the Matts

This recipe calls for St. Louis–style ribs because they have more meat and won't dry out while cooking. If you can't find them, use baby back ribs instead. It's highly recommended that you let them sit in the spice mix overnight, but they could go right into the oven. For the slaw, if you would like to cut the sharp onion flavor, soak the sliced red onions in cold water for 30 minutes. Drain and use as called for in the recipe.

Pork Carnitas with Grilled Mexican-Style Corn Casserole and Guacamole

MAKES 6 SERVINGS

This checks all the boxes of my game-day food requirements: It's gonna feed a lot of people. It's gonna bring the flavor. And I don't have to do a damn thing once it's all laid out on the table.

Pro Move

For a little extra somethin', you can deep-fry the pork once it's cooled to get it crispy on the outside.

To make the carnitas: In a Dutch oven or large, deep pot, stir together the cola, whole milk, yellow onion, orange, garlic cloves, salt, and pepper. Add the pork, cover, and let marinate in the fridge for 2 hours.

Preheat the oven to 375°F.

Add the vegetable oil to the pork mixture and cover the pot with aluminum foil. Bake the pork for 3 hours, or until it is tender and falling apart. Keep warm.

To make the corn casserole: While the carnitas roast, lightly coat a 9 by 13-inch casserole dish with nonstick cooking spray and set aside.

In a large bowl, gently stir together the corn, mayo, sour cream, ¾ cup of the Cotija, Monterey Jack, cilantro, sugar, lime juice, salt, and pepper. Transfer the mixture to the prepared casserole dish and

continued ▶

PORK CARNITAS

1 (12-ounce) can Coca-Cola

¾ cup whole milk

½ yellow onion, sliced

½ navel orange, cut into 1-inch pieces

5 garlic cloves

3 tablespoons kosher salt

1 tablespoon freshly ground black pepper

5 pounds boneless pork butt, cut into 3-inch pieces

6 cups vegetable oil (see Note)

GRILLED MEXICAN-STYLE CORN CASSEROLE

6 cups frozen grilled or roasted corn, thawed (see Note)

1 cup mayonnaise

1 cup sour cream

1 cup crumbled Cotija cheese

½ cup shredded Monterey Jack cheese

⅓ cup chopped fresh cilantro

¼ cup granulated sugar

2 tablespoons fresh lime juice

1 tablespoon kosher salt

1 teaspoon freshly ground black pepper

Pork Carnitas with Grilled Mexican-Style Corn Casserole and Guacamole

CONTINUED

GUACAMOLE

5 avocados, cubed

½ cup chopped fresh cilantro

¼ cup finely diced red onion

¼ cup fresh lime juice

2 tablespoons minced jalapeño chile (seeded for less heat)

2 tablespoons chipotle-flavored hot sauce (preferably Tabasco)

2 tablespoons extra-virgin olive oil

2 teaspoons kosher salt

1 teaspoon freshly ground black pepper

1 teaspoon garlic powder

Warmed tortillas for serving

top with the remaining ¼ cup Cotija. Cover the dish with foil and bake with the carnitas for 45 minutes. Remove the foil and bake for 15 minutes more, or until bubbly and beginning to brown around the edges.

To make the guacamole: While the casserole is cooking, in a medium bowl, combine the avocado, cilantro, red onion, lime juice, jalapeño, hot sauce, olive oil, salt, pepper, and garlic powder. Mix gently if you like it on the chunky side, or use a whisk to mix until smooth. Cover with plastic wrap, laying the plastic directly on the surface of the guacamole to keep it from turning brown. Set aside in the fridge.

Serve the carnitas with warmed tortillas, the corn casserole, and guacamole on the side.

Put Away and Replay

Store the carnitas, casserole, and guacamole in separate sealed containers in the fridge for up to 3 days. Reheat the carnitas and casserole in a microwave on high power for 2 minutes, or until heated through.

Notes from the Matts

For even more flavor, use lard instead of oil when cooking your carnitas. Same goes for grilling fresh corn, instead of using frozen, and cutting it off the cob for the corn casserole.

Shrimp Enchiladas with Green Sauce

MAKES 6 SERVINGS

GREEN SAUCE

2 (4-ounce) cans chopped mild green chiles, with juices

1 (4-ounce) can chopped hot green chiles, with juices

¼ cup unsalted butter

¼ cup all-purpose flour

3 (12-ounce) cans evaporated milk

1 cup sour cream

2 teaspoons kosher salt

1 teaspoon freshly ground black pepper

1 teaspoon garlic powder

½ teaspoon onion powder

½ teaspoon ground cumin

½ teaspoon dried oregano

½ cup chopped fresh cilantro

¼ cup extra-virgin olive oil

1 yellow onion, finely diced

1 large red bell pepper, seeded and diced

½ cup finely diced poblano chile

2 pounds 31/40 shrimp, peeled and chopped into thirds

2 tablespoons minced jalapeño chile (seeded for less heat)

There's a reason people say things are the "whole enchilada," because they've got everything you could possibly want and need. These little shrimp-filled guys live up to their namesake in every way.

To make the green sauce: In a blender, combine the mild and hot green chiles with their juices and puree until smooth. Set aside.

In a medium pot over low heat, melt the butter. Add the flour and whisk constantly for 1 to 2 minutes to cook the flour. Add the green chile puree, evaporated milk, sour cream, salt, black pepper, garlic powder, onion powder, cumin, and oregano and stir well to eliminate any lumps. Turn the heat to medium and bring the mixture to a boil. Cook for about 4 minutes, or until the sauce thickens slightly. Remove from the heat and stir in the cilantro. Set aside.

Preheat the oven to 350°F. Line a rimmed baking dish with aluminum foil and set aside.

In a large, deep pan over medium-high heat, warm the olive oil. Add the onion, bell pepper, and poblano and cook for 3 to 4 minutes, or until the onion is translucent. Add the shrimp, jalapeño, and minced garlic and cook for 3 minutes more, or until the shrimp just start to turn pink. (They'll finish cooking in the oven.) Remove the pan from the heat and stir in the butter, salt, black pepper, and chipotle powder. Set the mixture aside to cool to room temperature. Once cooled, stir in 4 cups of the Monterey Jack and the cilantro.

continued ▶

Shrimp Enchiladas with Green Sauce

CONTINUED

2 tablespoons minced garlic

2 tablespoons unsalted butter

2 teaspoons kosher salt

1 teaspoon freshly ground black pepper

½ teaspoon chipotle powder

6 cups shredded Monterey Jack cheese

½ cup chopped fresh cilantro

18 (6-inch) corn tortillas

Wrap the tortillas in a damp kitchen towel and microwave them on high power for 2 minutes to soften.

Spread a layer of the green sauce on the bottom of the prepared baking dish. Divide the shrimp mixture evenly among the tortillas, wrap each tortilla around the filling, and place in the sauce, seam-side down. Do your best to wrap each one fairly tight, so the filling stays inside, and so there's enough room for every enchilada in the baking dish. Once all the enchiladas are nestled together, top with most of the remaining green sauce. (You'll want some left to serve at the table.) Top with the remaining 2 cups cheese and bake for 30 minutes, or until all the cheese is melted and the filling is hot.

Serve the enchiladas straight from the oven with the remaining sauce on the side.

Put Away and Replay

Store the enchiladas in an airtight container in the fridge for up to 2 days. Reheat, uncovered, in a 350°F oven, for about 25 minutes, or until heated through.

Note from the Matts

You can substitute fresh or frozen and thawed crab or lobster for the shrimp.

"Excellence is not a singular act, but a habit. You are what you repeatedly do."

7

IT AIN'T OVER 'TIL THERE'S

BANANA PUDDING

dessert!

If so many people weren't expecting to find the dessert recipes last, I'd say this chapter should really be the first one in the book. That's because growing up, we never had dessert; we couldn't afford it.

So, I always said if I ever made it big, I was going to eat dessert first. And now I do. But no matter how successful I've been, I've always respected the humble roots of my favorite sweet things. You can keep your foo-foo crème brûlée and your bread pudding. (Why would you eat that? Is it bread? Is it pudding?) For me it's all about the simple things like brownies, cobbler, doughnuts, and, of course, homemade banana pudding, just like my mother taught me how to make it.

Banana Pudding

MAKES 8 SERVINGS

Growing up, this was one of the few recipes I'd make with my mother, and she made it all the time, so I'm what you could call a pudding specialist. I know how to get the cookie layers just right—some in the middle, some on the top; so the crispy-cookie people and soggy-cookie people will all be happy—and that you gotta eat it when it's cold. Honestly, if desserts were basketball players, banana pudding would be the all-star, championship winner, Olympic Gold Medal-winner, Hall of Famer, MVP.

Pro Move

Mama O'Neal was all about the instant vanilla pudding, but we're gonna take things up just a notch by making it from scratch. If you happen to sneak one of those packets into the recipe, I won't tell anyone.

2 (12-ounce) cans evaporated milk

1½ cups granulated sugar

1 cup chopped bananas and 3 cups sliced bananas (about 6 bananas; see Note)

⅓ cup plus 2 tablespoons all-purpose flour

1 teaspoon vanilla extract

½ teaspoon table salt

6 egg yolks

¼ cup unsalted butter, cut into ½-inch pieces

4 cups vanilla wafers

Canned whipped cream for serving (see Note)

In a blender, combine the evaporated milk, sugar, chopped bananas, flour, vanilla, and salt and blend until smooth. Pour the mixture into a large, deep sauté pan over medium heat. Cook, stirring constantly with a heatproof spatula, for 10 to 12 minutes, or until the mixture comes to a low boil and is very thick. Remove the pan from the heat and whisk in the egg yolks, followed by the butter, whisking quickly and constantly, so the yolks don't scramble. Fold in 3 cups of the wafers and the sliced bananas.

continued ▶

Banana Pudding

Transfer the pudding to a 9 by 13-inch casserole dish. Cover with plastic wrap, laying the plastic directly on the surface of the pudding to prevent a skin from forming. Chill the pudding for 3 to 4 hours or, ideally, overnight, until firm.

Chop the remaining 1 cup wafers. Sprinkle the pudding with the chopped wafers and serve with a squirt of whipped cream.

Put Away and Replay
Store the pudding in a sealed container in the fridge for up to 3 days.

Notes from the Matts

Try to get bananas that have a green tip, so not too ripe. If you prefer to skip the canned whipped cream and whip your own, use 1 cup heavy cream and 1 teaspoon powdered sugar. Whip until stiff peaks form.

Coffee-and-Doughnut Bake with Peanut Butter–Dulce de Leche

MAKES 8 SERVINGS

The thing with doughnuts is that you can never eat just one, or two. If you eat one or two, then there's gonna be a three or four, then five and six, seven and eight. And you think, *Well, there's only four left; might as well polish these off too.* You could say I'm a little bit of a doughnut aficionado and, as the owner of a Krispy Kreme in Atlanta and the global spokesperson for the brand, I officially give this dessert my stamp of approval.

To make the dulce de leche: Peel the paper labels off the cans of sweetened condensed milk. In a stockpot, place the cans on their sides and cover with 2 inches or more of water. Set the pot over high heat and bring to a boil. Turn the heat to low and cover the pot. Simmer for 2½ hours, periodically checking to make sure that the cans stay submerged and adding more hot water as needed. Using tongs, carefully remove the cans and let sit at room temperature to cool for 1 hour.

Empty the cans into a small saucepan over low heat, using a rubber spatula to really get every last bit out. Add the peanut butter and cook, stirring frequently, for about 2 minutes, just until combined and warm. Cover, remove the pot from the heat, and set aside.

To make the bake: While the sweetened condensed milk simmers, preheat the oven to 350°F. Lightly coat a 9 by 13-inch casserole dish with nonstick cooking spray and set aside.

continued ▶

PEANUT BUTTER–DULCE DE LECHE

2 (14-ounce) cans sweetened condensed milk

½ cup creamy peanut butter

COFFEE-AND-DOUGHNUT BAKE

12 eggs

2 (12-ounce) cans evaporated milk

¼ cup packed light brown sugar

3 tablespoons instant coffee

1 teaspoon vanilla extract

16 glazed cake donuts, cut into ½-inch pieces

1 cup dark chocolate chunks

Coffee-and-Doughnut Bake with Peanut Butter–Dulce de Leche

CONTINUED

In a large bowl, whisk together the eggs, evaporated milk, brown sugar, instant coffee, and vanilla. Fold in the doughnut pieces and chocolate, coating them evenly in the batter. Transfer the mixture to the prepared dish, cover with aluminum foil, and bake for 1½ hours. Remove the foil and continue baking for 10 to 25 minutes, or until the center of the bake is firm to the touch. Let the bake cool slightly for 5 minutes.

Rewarm the dulce de leche over low heat, if needed.

Serve the coffee-and-doughnut bake warm, drizzled with the peanut butter–dulce de leche.

Put Away and Replay
Store the bake and dulce de leche in separate sealed containers in the fridge for up to 3 days. Microwave each on high power for 1 to 2 minutes, or until warm.

Notes from the Matts

For the dulce de leche, you can keep the unopened cans of cooked milk at room temperature for up to 1 month. Once you open them, they need to be refrigerated and used. Dulce de leche also makes a great topping for ice cream and Oreo Cookie Brownie Sundaes (page 215), among other things. For the doughnut bake, feel free to use milk chocolate instead of dark.

Frosted Flakes–Chocolate Chip Cookies

MAKES ABOUT 24 COOKIES

As I said before, me and Tony the Tiger go way back. After I won my first championship, Wheaties asked me to be on the box. But when I was a kid, we couldn't afford Wheaties. So, I became a Frosted Flakes guy. And let me tell you, I've never looked back. I always have a box around, ready for that late-night snack attack.

Preheat the oven to 350°F. Lightly coat two baking sheets with nonstick cooking spray and set aside.

In a stand mixer fitted with the paddle attachment, cream together the butter, brown sugar, and granulated sugar on high speed for 3 minutes. Scrape down the bowl once or twice with a spatula if needed to make sure all the ingredients get combined. Add the egg and vanilla and continue beating on high speed for 8 minutes, scraping down the sides of the bowl if needed.

In a medium bowl, combine the flour, salt, baking powder, and baking soda. With the mixer on low speed, add the dry ingredients to the butter mixture and mix just until incorporated, 30 seconds to 1 minute. Using a spatula or spoon, gently fold in the Frosted Flakes and chocolate chips.

continued ▶

1 cup unsalted butter, at room temperature

1 cup packed light brown sugar

½ cup granulated sugar

1 egg

1 teaspoon vanilla extract

1¼ cups all-purpose flour

1 teaspoon table salt

½ teaspoon baking powder

¼ teaspoon baking soda

3 cups Frosted Flakes cereal

2 cups semisweet chocolate chips

Frosted Flakes–Chocolate Chip Cookies

CONTINUED

Using a medium ice-cream scoop or ¼-cup measure, scoop the dough onto the prepared baking sheets, leaving about 2 inches between each mound. Bake the cookies for 15 to 17 minutes, or until lightly browned. Transfer the cookies to a wire rack to cool before serving.

Put Away and Replay
Store the cookies in an airtight container at room temperature for up to 1 week.

Note from the Matts

You can make this dough ahead and store it in an airtight container in the fridge for up to 24 hours before baking.

Oreo Cookie Brownie Sundaes

MAKES 9 BROWNIES

It only makes sense that I love Oreos—dunking is in my DNA.
Normally, I keep things pretty classic with the no-frills cookie-
milk one-two; but every once in a while, you gotta leave some
room to freestyle, which is when I get a brownie sundae in the
mix too. You're gonna need a bigger spoon for this one.

Pro Moves

These are also great with Peanut Butter–Dulce de Leche
(see page 209), if you have any left over. If you have time to
make the brownies ahead, let them sit overnight in a sealed
container or resealable plastic bag—they're even better
the next day.

1 cup semisweet
chocolate chips

½ cup unsalted butter

26 Oreo cookies, plus
crumbled cookies for
sprinkling

4 eggs

1 cup cocoa powder

¾ cup packed
light brown sugar

½ cup granulated sugar

½ cup all-purpose flour

2 teaspoons vanilla extract

½ teaspoon table salt

Vanilla ice cream for serving

Preheat the oven to 325°F. Lightly coat a 9 by 9-inch baking dish
with nonstick cooking spray and set aside.

In a small microwave-safe bowl, combine the chocolate chips and
butter and microwave on high power for 30 seconds. Stir gently
and return the bowl to the microwave for 30 seconds more. Repeat
these intervals until the mixture is just melted. Set aside.

In a medium bowl, using the handle of a spoon, crush ten of the
Oreos. In a stand mixer fitted with the paddle attachment, beat
the eggs on high speed for 3 to 4 minutes, or until light and fluffy.
Add the melted chocolate mixture, crushed Oreos, cocoa powder,
brown sugar, granulated sugar, flour, vanilla, and salt; turn the
speed to low; and mix just until combined.

continued ▶

Oreo Cookie Brownie Sundaes

CONTINUED

Turn the batter out into the prepared baking dish, using a spatula to spread it out evenly. Chop the remaining sixteen Oreos and sprinkle them over the top in an even layer.

Bake the brownies for 30 to 35 minutes, or until a knife or toothpick inserted into the center of the brownies comes out clean. Let cool for 10 minutes before cutting into nine equal squares.

Serve the brownies topped with a scoop of ice cream and sprinkled with crumbled cookies.

Put Away and Replay
Store the brownies in a sealed container at room temperature for up to 2 days. Microwave on high power for 1 minute, if you prefer them warm.

Note from the Matts

You can add ½ cup chopped nuts and/or ½ cup chocolate chips to the brownies, folding them in once the batter is mixed, if you want to add more texture.

Whiskey-Peach Cobbler
with Cinnamon-Maple Whipped Cream

MAKES 8 SERVINGS

Used to be that the only pies I knew a thing or two about were pizza pies, like the Shaq-a-Roni that I came up with for Papa John's. But then I met a cobbler; and let me tell you, a cobbler is basically just a pie casserole that I take to the next level with some whiskey (though you can leave it out). You still get that nice buttery, flaky thing happening on the top, but no need for messing with rolling pins or fancy equipment.

To make the cobbler: Preheat the oven to 350°F. Lightly coat a 9 by 13-inch casserole dish with nonstick cooking spray and set aside.

In a small pot over medium heat, melt ½ cup of the butter with the brown sugar. Bring the mixture to a simmer and carefully stir in the whiskey (if using). (It might flame. If it does, stand back and let the flames die out naturally; or if the flame is really large, cover the pan with another pan, inverted, to extinguish.) Cook for 3 minutes, or until the alcohol has burned off. Set aside to cool.

In a large bowl, toss together the peaches, cornstarch, cinnamon, vanilla, ½ teaspoon of the salt, and nutmeg (if using). Pour the butter mixture over the peaches and fold gently to combine. Transfer the peach mixture to the prepared casserole dish.

continued ▶

WHISKEY-PEACH COBBLER

1 cup unsalted butter

1 cup packed light brown sugar

½ cup whiskey (optional)

10 cups frozen sliced peaches (see Note)

3 tablespoons cornstarch

2 teaspoons ground cinnamon

1 teaspoon vanilla extract

1 teaspoon table salt

⅛ teaspoon ground nutmeg (optional)

2 cups all-purpose flour

½ cup granulated sugar

1½ teaspoons baking powder

¼ teaspoon baking soda

¾ cup buttermilk

CINNAMON-MAPLE WHIPPED CREAM

2 cups heavy cream, cold

¼ cup maple syrup

¼ cup powdered sugar

1 teaspoon ground cinnamon

½ teaspoon maple extract

Whiskey-Peach Cobbler with Cinnamon-Maple Whipped Cream

Cut the remaining ½ cup butter into ½-inch pieces. In a medium bowl, whisk together the flour, granulated sugar, baking powder, baking soda, and remaining ½ teaspoon salt. Add the cubed butter and work it into the flour mixture with your hands until it's in very small, pea-size pieces. Stir in the buttermilk until the mixture forms a rough dough. Flatten handful-size pieces of the dough between your thumb and forefinger and place them over the filling. It's okay to have some of the filling still showing through. Cover the baking dish with aluminum foil and bake for 1 hour 20 minutes. Remove the foil and bake for 25 minutes more.

To make the whipped cream: While the cobbler bakes, in the bowl of a stand mixer fitted with the whisk attachment, or using a handheld mixer, combine the heavy cream, maple syrup, powdered sugar, cinnamon, and maple extract and whip until stiff peaks form. Cover and set aside in the refrigerator.

Serve the cobbler warm, spooned into bowls and topped with dollops of the whipped cream.

Put Away and Replay

Store the cobbler in a sealed container at room temperature for up to 3 days. Store the whipped cream, covered tightly, in the fridge for up to 2 days. Microwave the cobbler on high power for 1 minute, or until hot.

Note from the Matts

You can substitute berries for the peaches, or blend fruits together for the cobbler filling.

"I'll start my diet tomorrow."

Hummingbird Pineapple Upside-Down Bundt Cake

MAKES 8 SERVINGS

1¾ cups all-purpose flour

1 cup granulated sugar

1 teaspoon table salt

1 teaspoon ground cinnamon

½ teaspoon baking soda

2 eggs

¾ cup canola oil

½ cup canned crushed pineapple, with juices

1 teaspoon vanilla extract

2 ripe bananas, sliced

½ cup chopped pecans

CREAM CHEESE GLAZE

1 cup powdered sugar

4 ounces plain cream cheese, at room temperature

⅓ cup 2% milk

¼ cup unsalted butter, at room temperature

1 teaspoon vanilla extract

½ teaspoon grated orange zest

Frankly, I think this could be called the Shaq Special Upside-Down Dunk Cake, but whenever you've got pineapple and cream cheese anything, you're gonna have a winner.

Preheat the oven to 350°F. Generously coat a 10-cup Bundt pan or 10-inch cake pan with nonstick cooking spray, flour lightly, and set aside.

In a large bowl, whisk together the 1¾ cups flour, granulated sugar, salt, cinnamon, and baking soda. In a medium bowl, whisk together the eggs, canola oil, pineapple with juices, and vanilla. Pour the wet ingredients over the dry ingredients and mix well. Fold in the bananas and pecans and transfer the batter to the prepared pan.

Bake the cake for 55 minutes, or until a toothpick inserted into the center comes out clean. Let the cake cool on a wire rack for 10 minutes, then turn onto a serving plate and let sit for 15 minutes.

To make the glaze: In a medium bowl, combine the powdered sugar, cream cheese, 2% milk, butter, vanilla, and orange zest and beat well with a handheld mixer until smooth.

Pour half of the glaze over the cooled cake. Cut the cake and serve with the remaining glaze on the side.

Put Away and Replay

Store the cake and glaze in separate sealed containers in the fridge for up to 3 days. Let come to room temperature before serving.

The Postgame Show

You didn't think I'd let this whole cookbook game go down without a little wrap-up, did you? That's what I do—I watch the plays, take it all in, then break it down for the people at home. I have no problem Shaqtin' the fool on national television. So, let's take a look at what you did here. You whisked, you marinated, you griddled, you casseroled, you sprinkled little bits of this and that, and put some top-notch meals on the table. I'm willing to bet that you made your family proud; or, at the very least, filled 'em up enough to make it to the next round of the homemade dinner versus delivery playoffs. Maybe it wasn't all barbecue chicken all the time, and maybe you didn't hit as many 3-pointers as you'd like, but you just need to keep putting in the reps—which is what being a player is all about, on the court and in the kitchen. Just know that me and these recipes got your back. And, if all else fails, there's always Papa John's.

'Til next time,

Shaquille

Acknowledgments

Much like the perfect play, it takes a whole lot of teammates to make a cookbook. High-fives and heartfelt thanks go to these MBAs.

My incredible mother, Lucille. These recipes are her heart and soul, and in writing this book we were able to bring back so many incredible childhood memories that we shared around the table with my sisters, Ayesha and Lateefah.

My beautiful children, Taahirah, Myles, Shareef, Amirah, Shaquir, and Me'arah. Everything I do is for all of you. Remember to keep your head down and work hard.

To my partners Authentic Brands Group and PRP, your relentless pursuit of perfection and ability to bring my ideas to fruition never cease to amaze me. Thank you for your support, friendship, encouragement, and willingness to try anything.

Matthew Silverman and Matthew Piekarski, this book simply would not have been possible without you, your attention to detail, and our shared love of all things delicious (and fried!).

Food writer Rachel Holtzman, you hit all the shots.

Photographer Eva Kolenko and food stylist Lillian Kang, you were the dream team.

Ten Speed Press Editor in Chief Lorena Jones ran point and brought the book-publishing A-team: Publisher Aaron Wehner, Deputy Creative Director Emma Campion, Designer Annie Marino, Production Design Manager Mari Gill, Senior Managing Editor Doug Ogan, Associate Production Editor Sohayla Farman, Production Manager Dan Myers, Marketing Director Windy Dorresteyn, Assistant Marketing Director Stephanie Davis, Publicity Director Kate Tyler, and Associate Publicity Director Jana Branson.

Index

Text copyright © 2022 by Shaq™ and Shaquille O'Neal™
Rights of Publicity and Persona Rights: ABG-Shaq, LLC.
Photographs copyright © 2022 by Eva Kolenko.

All rights reserved.

Published in the United States by Ten Speed Press, an imprint of Random House,
a division of Penguin Random House LLC, New York.
www.tenspeed.com

Ten Speed Press and the Ten Speed Press colophon are registered trademarks of
Penguin Random House LLC.

Library of Congress Cataloging-in-Publication Data
    Names: O'Neal, Shaquille, author.
    Title: Shaq's family style : championship recipes for feeding family and friends /
        Shaquille O'Neal with Rachel Holtzman, Matthew Silverman, and
        Matthew Piekarski.
    Description: First edition. | New York : Ten Speed Press, an imprint of Random
        House, a division of Penguin Random House LLC, [2022] |
    Includes index.
    Identifiers: LCCN 2021013056 (print) | LCCN 2021013057 (ebook) | ISBN
        9781984860064 (hardcover) | ISBN 9781984860071 (ebook)
    Subjects: LCSH: Cooking. | LCGFT: Cookbooks.
    Classification: LCC TX714 .O5493 2022 (print) | LCC TX714 (ebook) |
        DDC 641.5—dc23
    LC record available at https://lccn.loc.gov/2021013056
    LC ebook record available at https://lccn.loc.gov/2021013057

Hardcover ISBN: 978-1-9848-6006-4
eBook ISBN: 978-1-9848-6007-1

Printed in China

Editor: Lorena Jones | Production editors: Doug Ogan and Sohayla Farman
Designer: Annie Marino | Art director: Emma Campion
Production designers: Mari Gill and Faith Hague
Production manager: Dan Myers | Prepress color manager: Jane Chinn
Food stylist: Lillian Kang | Food stylist assistant: Paige Arnett
Main prop stylist: Claire Mack | Prop stylist assistant: Alyssa Kreidt
Location prop stylist: Charlotte Autry | Location prop assistant: Sean Rahill
First photo assistant: Brad Knilans | Location photo assistants: Fabio Atehortua and Roly Diaz
Photo re-toucher: Tammy White
Wardrobe stylist: Renee Brown | Personal stylist: Gena Sullivan
Hand models: Anthony Heaven, Charnell McQueen, Alyssa Kreidt
Copyeditor: Mary Cassells | Proofreader: Adaobi Obi Tulton | Indexer: Ken DellaPenta
Publicists: Kate Tyler and Jana Branson | Marketers: Windy Dorresteyn and Stephanie Davis

10 9 8 7 6 5 4 3 2 1

First Edition